Yiddish Sayings Mama Never Taught You

An Authors Guild Backinprint.com Edition
Published by iUniverse, Inc.

iUniverse books may be ordered through booksellers or by contacting:

iUniverse
1663 Liberty Drive
Bloomington, IN 47403
www.iuniverse.com
1-800-Authors (1-800-288-4677)

Because of the dynamic nature of the Internet, any Web addresses or links
contained in this book may have changed since publication and may no longer be
valid.

ISBN: 978-1-4401-4016-7 (pbk)

Printed in the United States of America

iUniverse rev. date: 4/22/2009

Yiddish Sayings

MAMA NEVER TAUGHT YOU
by
WELTMAN & ZUCKERMAN

An Authors Guild Backinprint.com Edition

iUniverse, Inc.
New York   Bloomington

יודישע

שפריכווערטער און רעדענסארטען

געזאמעלט און דערקלערט

פון

איגנאץ בערנשטיין.

(איבעלאסענע אין ראבע שפריכווערטער).

1908.

"... the town wits are reminded of stories not quite decorous, at which the men stroke their beards and smile, and the older women rebuke the wags, not too seriously, while the young matrons turn their faces away, only to look back furtively and giggle."

——Mendele Mocher Seforim,
Benjamin the Third (1885)

CONTENTS

INTRODUCTION

The several hundred "coarse and erotic" sayings present-
ed here were translated and transliterated by the editors
from the original Yiddish text. These folk expressions come
directly from the Jewish **shtetl**-community, as it existed
before the turn of the century.[1] Because of this, they
give us a valuable view of the **shtetl** in its prime, before it
was decimated by emigration, and ripped by revolution,
war and Holocaust. More important, the sayings illuminate
aspects of **shtetl** life which are almost entirely neglected by
current literary and academic sources. By this we mean the
life of the streets and the markets, of the **proste mentshn**
(common people), of the thieves, whores, and pimps, and,
to a large extent, of the usually upright citizens in their
occasional crudities, infidelities, and impieties.

The sayings themselves were collected by the folklorist
Ignaz Bernstein, as part of a monumental survey of Jewish
proverbs and folksayings. That remarkable source book,
Leksikon fun der Nayer Yidisher Literatur [2] (Dictionary
of Modern Yiddish Literature), gives us the background of
Bernstein and his work. We excerpt from it here, in English
translation, with grateful acknowledgement:

> Ignaz Bernstein (1836-1909) was born in
> Vinitse, Ukraine. His father was a rich sugar
> manufacturer and a great philanthropist.

---

[1] **Shtetl** generally refers to the Jewish small town or hamlet of
Eastern Europe. But life was lived so similarly in the big cities, that
shtetl-community will describe almost any tight-knit Jewish com-
munity of the period.

[2] Congress for Jewish Culture, Inc., N.Y., 1956, Vol. 1, p. 407.

The family settled in Warsaw in 1856. In 1859, Bernstein was in Berlin, and accidentally came upon a collection of Jewish proverbs. These interested him so much that he began to collect Jewish proverbs and related literature. He collected 4,780 examples in 100 languages. In 1900, Bernstein published a two-volume catalogue of his collection. It is considered one of the few typographical masterworks. He left this collection as an endowment to the Polish Academy of Science in Cracow, which, out of "gratitude," did not even mention his name in its biographical lexicon. In 1908, a luxury edition was published in Leipzig of **Yiddish Proverbs and Sayings**, in the original Yiddish, with a transliteration into the Roman alphabet, including annotations and explanations, a key in Yiddish, and a glossary of the Hebrew words translated into German. Benjamin Segal and Dr. Shmuel Poznanski assisted him in the work of that publication. That monumental and epochal publication was "Dedicated to the Jewish People" and comprises almost 4000 proverbs. Also in 1908, Bernstein published 227 obscene proverbs under the title "Erotica and Rustica," which later was reprinted twice. Bernstein died in Brussels and his body was returned for burial to Warsaw.

It is apparent that Bernstein kept his 227 examples of "Erotica and Rustica" out of his major work and published them separately in the same year (1908). A good question is, "Why?" On the flyleaf of the original book appears the following, in German: "als manuskript gedruckt" (printed as a manuscript). What "printed as a manuscript" actually means, we cannot say positively. But in all probability it refers to what we call in English a "privately printed" or "limited" edition. Did his publisher protest the nature of this material and ask that it be removed from the main body? Was Bernstein himself fearful of public reaction? Most likely it was meant, at least in part, as a demurrer, a notice that while these examples might be of some interest, he, Bernstein, had the sensitivity not to publish them abroad, to the world at large, but only in "working form" to the select few.

In any case, these **proste** (coarse) relatives of Bernstein's respected proverb family remained little known and untranslated for nearly 70 years, until they were brought to our attention by a good friend, who happened to own one of the original volumes. The sayings led us first to enjoyment, as we chuckled over this earthy glimpse of our forefathers' world, then to consternation, as we struggled to translate them into some recognizable present day-equivalent. Has there ever been a translator who has not asked dispensation for his demanding and pre-doomed labors?

The famous American poetess, Marianne Moore, translator of La Fontaine's **Fables,** put it this way: "The first requisite of a translation is that it should not sound like a translation." With this we agree wholeheartedly. We purposefully avoided Molly Goldberg "Yinglish"; we wanted to express as accurately as possible the sense and rhythm of these old Yiddish sayings in a contemporary American idiom, which was not too hot, and not too mild. In this we think we have succeeded. However, we do not deceive ourselves that we have succeeded entirely. Robert Frost once said, "poetry is that which cannot be translated." And much of these sayings — scatology and obscenity aside — may be termed poetic, for so many of them employ all the devices employed by poets: concision, pith, rhyme, rhythm, alliteration, consonance, internal rhyme, assonance, and word-play.

If you know Yiddish at all, and if you want some idea of the difficulties we encountered, try your own hand at translating the samples below, then look at our version.

You will become in this way more charitable, and perhaps even pleasantly surprised at our occasional happy hits:

- . *Kleyne kinder kakn kleyne kupkelakh.*
- . *Der kleyner iz on beyner, un ale beyner kumen fun im aroys.*
- . *Gots vinder, a puts makht kinder.*

As Henry Miller stated in a personal note to us: "I found the original Yiddish so much more juicy, savoury, spicy than the English — no fault of the translators." We couldn't agree more; we can only say we did our best.

The English transliteration, which accompanies the translation, puts the original Yiddish within reach of those who cannot cope with Hebrew characters. [3] Readers with a speaking, or more likely a listening, knowledge of Yiddish will be able to appreciate fully the richness of expression. But even non-Yiddish speakers, like Henry Miller, will be surprised at how much of the language they grasp. For the rules of transliteration, we adopted the YIVO [4] convention. This we did not only to help YIVO in its effort to standardize the transliteration of Yiddish, but also to convey the Yiddish sounds as accurately and as consistently as possible.

The YIVO system is not without its shortcomings. For example, the sounds "ee" and "ih" are both rendered by "i"; and to an American, "kh" is not immediately understood as the sound of "ch" in the German **ach** or the

---

[3] The Yiddish used in this book is photographically reproduced from the original Bernstein edition of 1908.

[4] YIVO is an acronym for **Yidishe Visnshaftlikhe Institut** (Yiddish Scientific Institute), now called "YIVO Institute for Jewish Research." Founded in Vilno in 1925, and since 1941 based in New York, it is the only secular Jewish research institute outside Israel, and is dedicated to the scholarly exploration of all phases of Jewish life.

Scottish **loch**. But although **Khanike** or **Khassidic** may seem strange (we're used to seeing **Chanukah** and **Chassidic**, or **Hannuka** and **Hassidic**), "kh" is preferable to "ch" which can stand for **k** or **tsh**, as in **Christmas** or **church**, but never for the uvular/gutteral sound required by Yiddish. And "kh" is certainly preferable to "h" which makes no sense whatsoever. Here are some other essentials of the YIVO system which need explanation:

ey is pronounced as the **ey** in **grey**.
ay is pronounced as the **i** in **fine**.
 i is pronounced as the **i** in **fit**, or
    as the **ee** in **seed**.

While we tried to follow Bernstein as closely as possible in matters of translation and transliteration, we did make one major change in his presentation. This was in the order of the sayings. In the original edition, the sayings are arranged in strict alphabetical order, numbered, with Bernstein's occasional explications and etymological notes printed small below them. We included most of Bernstein's comments, adding our own where we thought his were inadequate or off the mark. But we also created nine categories for the sayings, arranging them within these according to certain apparent or underlying similarities or contrasts, often in such a way that the sayings begin to sound like a sort of "folk dialogue." The nine categories turned out as follows:

1. Coming of Age
2. Women of Virtue and Otherwise
3. Men About Town
4. The Marriage Bed
5. The Crux of the Matter
6. Eat and Be Well
7. Getting Old
8. Talmudic Takeoffs
9. Wit and Wisdom

The new arrangement gives the sayings a sense of life that they sometimes lost in Bernstein's rather Teutonic format.

In addition to our own comments (marked by "(eds.)"), we have included Bernstein's, both in the original Yiddish, and in translation (marked by an "(i.b.)" in the text). Very often Bernstein's explication struck us as just as funny, or funnier, than the saying. For example:

> *Who doesn't lust for the tip of the bust?*
> One means here, of course, the womanly bust. (i.b.)

or,

> *When you sleep with your wife, you show your behind to the world.*
> What this refers to is the position of the man during intercourse. (i.b.)

The first comment is superfluous; the second focuses on the literal meaning, missing the implied one altogether. Their naivete and literalness are endearing.

But technicalities aside, how do we face the question of Yiddish obscenity. Dirty Yiddish. Who ever heard of dirty Yiddish? My **bobe** talking dirty? Bite your tongue! Well, for one thing, most of the expressions aren't so dirty after all. Or rather, we do not react to the Yiddish words as strongly as we do to some of their English equivalents. **Tokhes, shmuk, kakn, pishn,** and those delightful indirections **pirog, futer, taytl, baytl,** and **der kleyner,** while earthy enough, just don't seem as obscene to us in Yiddish as do their English counterparts.

We have some theories as to why that should be, but are at a loss for a completely satisfactory explanation. It may be because, ourselves being raised in a refined Yiddishist environment, we did not learn such words early in a "dirty" context, where they would have partaken fully of the intended "dirty" connotations. Or it may be because many of these "obscene" terms in Yiddish are used in situations where they would be taboo or offensive in English. An ordinary **shtetl** mother might use **tokhes** and and **pishn** in scolding or joking with her child; an American middle-class mother would not use **ass** or **piss** with her children, unless inordinately provoked. This may be a linguistic reflection of the difference in Anglo-American attitudes toward bodily functions, as opposed to traditional Jewish ones. In fact, almost as many of these sayings have to do with elimination, with pissing, crapping and farting, as with sexual intercourse or sexual play. From this standpoint, it seems as if the later focus of American Jewish comedians on Yiddishe mamas, on constipation, and on the infirmities of old age, is not so far off the mark after all.

Another thing. Both shtetl **khokhme** (wisdom, cleverness) and shtetl **eydlkayt** (refinement, nobility) pervade these sayings, mitigating their coarse nature. They are not merely "dirty," they are also clever and witty. They are related to study-house **pilpul**[5] and to Talmudic bookishness. They are built on puns and word associations, on alliterations, and on logical inversions. Unfortunately, these very attributes of wit and intelligence are what often keep these sayings from coming off (no pun intended) in translation. The study house twist of logic or language, the pun and the rhyme, are the hardest things to convey in translation. The bare sense (again, no pun) is sometimes all that comes through, and that often isn't as funny by itself.

Finally, we see that even the most explicit sayings are totally without the edge of cruelty which we often find

[5] Talmudic argumentation; hair-splitting casuistry.

associated with sex in our culture. The speakers, who seem to be mainly men, are sometimes cutting, but more usually philosophical, even self-deprecating. And in the end, cruelty is perhaps the only real obscenity.

But to say that these expressions are only mildly dirty is not to say that publication of Bernstein's collection will now be welcomed with universal enthusiasm. Yiddishists — that loyal segment of East European Jewry who built an ideology, a national culture, and a social movement out of an attachment to a language — Yiddishists, who usually derive much pleasure from published translations of unknown Yiddish works, will, by and large, not like this book. We have already been served notice. It's not **eydl** (refined). It's bad for the Jews. Why **this** book? It's not nice. It shows Jews and Yiddish in a poor light.

But does it? Aren't Jews like other people? Isn't Yiddish a complete language, like any other? Why should **shtetl-folk** not be shown as full-blooded, hearty, earthy, natural, sexy, and coarse, as well as suffering and devout. Idyllic shtetl-nostalgia is badly in need of some naturalistic correctives. The Jewish people of Eastern Europe deserve to be shown in all their humanity, and that includes the part below the Khassidic **gartl** (belt), which seperates the divine upper half of the body from the mundane lower. Shall our East European Jews be remembered only as mild Bontches and saintly Tevyes, floating quaintly-costumed in a technicolor haze, living their life-is-with-people lives to snappy Broadway melodies?

No, of course not. And what's more, if these sayings reveal Jewish coarseness, scatology, and sexuality, they reveal them as, again, uniquely Jewish. Not just funny but punny, not just coarse but clever, not simply salacious but subtle, not only lewd but also lusty, full of life and laughter. American Jews, once, twice, or three times removed from their East European origins, will delight in discovering these earthy remnants of the vital, living culture from which they spring, and which, tragically, exists no more. And others, Jews and Gentiles alike, unless fettered by unremitting refinement, not to say prudery, will laugh and, if you permit us: enjoy, enjoy!

Gershon Weltman, Ph.D.
Marvin S. Zuckerman

1. COMING OF AGE

Er veyst shoyn, vos a meydl hot (oder. . .vos a meydl hot nit).

He already knows what little girls have (or. . .what little girls don't have).

    A boy who has discovered early all the secrets. (i.b.)

Ale meydlakh zenen psule, azoy lang der boykh shvaygt.

All girls are virgins, as long as their stomaches don't tell on them.

Az in der shtot iz do an eyruv, meg a meydl oykh trogn.

Since every town has an Eyruv, then a maiden may also carry.

    The Eyruv is a special border within which one is permitted to carry goods on the Sabbath. "To carry" is also to be pregnant. So. . .if even the Sabbath laws have dispensations, why not one for maidens? (eds.)

A meydl fun akhtsn yor meg shoyn trogn on an eyruv.

A girl of eighteen can carry without special permission.

Far shrek hot di moyd mapl gevezn.

Out of fright, the girl miscarried.

ער ווייסט שוין, וואס א מיידעל האט (אָדער ... וואס א מיידעל האט ניט.)
א ינגעל, וואס ער איז פֿריה געוואָהר געוואָרען פֿון אַלע סודות.

אַלע מיידלעך זענען בתולות, אַזוי לאַנג דער בויך שווייגט.

אַז אין דער שטאַדט איז דא אַן עירוב, מעג א מיידעל אויך טראָגען.

א מיידעל פֿון אכטצעהן יאָהר מעג שוין טראָגען אָהן אַן עירוב.

פֿאַר שרעק האָט די מויד מפיל געוואָרען.

3

Itlikher bokher iz a zokher, ober nit itlikher zokher iz a bokher.

Every boy is a male, but not every male is still a boy.

A bokher mit a zokher shayt zikh.

Keep the buds away from the studs.

> The reference is to homosexual passion. They still tell the anecdote about two good, long-time friends who agreed that there would be a marriage between their children. As it happened, however, both had boys. At this, the elders themselves realized that such a match would be impossible to consumate. (i.b.)

Kleyne kinder kakn kleyne kupkelekh.

Tiny tots make tiny turds.

> Children say this to learn hard-to-pronounce words. (i.b.)

Tsun'a guter kop muz men nokh hobn a gutn akhur.

To have a good head you also need a good butt.

> That is one must also have **zitsfleysh** (sit-ability) and be diligent. (i.b.)

4

איטליכער בָּחור איז אַ זָכָר, אָבָּער ניט איטליכער זָכָר איז אַ בָּחור.

אַ בָּחור מיט אַ זָכָר שיים זיך.

מָען מיינט די תּאַוה פון מִשְכַּב־זָכָר. — מָען דָערצָעהלט נָאך אן אַנעקדָאטע, אַז צְווַיי
אַלטע ניטע אָבְּריינד הָאבָּען צְווישען זיך אַבְּנָעבָּעדט אַ שידוך פַאר זַיערע צְווַיי קלַיינע
קינדָער. שפּעטָער הָאט זיך אָבָּער אַרויסגעשטעלם, אַז בַּיידע הָאבָּען נָעהָאט יונגלָעך.
דָא הָאבָּען די עלטָערן אַלַיין אַיינגָעזעהען, אַז אַזאַ שידוך איז ניט מָעגליך אויסצופיהרָען.

קלַיינע קינדָער בַּאקען קלַיינע קיפָּקֶעלָעך.

קיפָּקֶעלָע = p. kupka. — קינדָער נָעווָעהנָען זיך דָערטים שטָערע ווָערטֶער
אַרויסצוריידָען.

צוריקלאַ נוטען[?] קָאפּ מוז מָען נָאך הָאבָּען אַ נוטען אָחור.
ד. ה. מָען מיז נָאך הָאבָּען זיצְפלַיש און זַיין פלַייסיג.

Gib tokhes un gey varemes esn.

Present your behind and have your lunch hot.

> So says the **kheyder** (elementary school) teacher's assistant to the kheyder-boys, whenever he whips them before letting them go home to eat their lunches. (i.b.)

Fraytik, iz der tokhes tsaytik.

Friday, and the behind is ready.

> For spanking, that is — it is a custom in the Jewish schools to spank the boys on Friday regardless, so that they will remember over the Sabbath. Besides this, one means sexual intercourse on Friday night, when every man observes **oyneg shabes** (the delight of the Sabbath). (i.b.)

A b'sulo meg men shoyfekh dam zayn, ober nor in der ershter nakht.

You may shed a maiden's blood, but only on the first night.

A meydl iz ibrik oyf a bris, ober tsum bris makhn muz zi zayn derbay.

You don't need a girl at a circumcision, but to have one you can't do without her.

גיב תָּחָת אוּן נֶעה וַואַרעֶמעֶם עֶסעֶן.

אַזוֹי זָאגט דער בַּעלפֿער צו די חָדֶר־יוּנגלעֶך, אַז עֶר שמַייסט זֵיי אָב, אַידער עֶר לָאזט
זֵיי אַהֵיים נֶעהָען צו וואַרעֶמעֶם (מיטאָן עֶסעֶן.)

פֿרַייטָאג. אין דעֶר תָּחָת צֵייטִן.

ד. ה. צום אָפּשמַייסעֶן. — עֶס איז אין די חַדָרִים אַ מִנהָג, די יוּנגלעֶן סַיַי וִוי סַיַי
פֿרַייטָאג אָפּצושמַייסעֶן, כְּדֵי זֵיי זָאלעֶן עֶס געֶדעֶנקעֶן איבער שַבָּת. — הוּץ דעֶם מֵיינט מעֶן
דעֶם תַּשׁמִישׁ הַמִטָה פֿרַייטָאג־צו־נאַכטס, וָואס אִיטלעֶכער יוד הַאלט עֶס אַלט אָן אָן עֶנע שַבָּת.

אַ בְּתוּלָה מעֶן מעֶן שוֹפֵךְ דַם זַיין, אָבֶּער נָאר אין דעֶר עֶרשטעֶר נאַכט.

אַ מֵיידעֶל אִיז אִיבּרִין אוֹיף אַ בְּרִית. אָבָּער צום בְּרִית מוּז מאַכעֶן מוּ זַיין
דעֶרבַּיי.

A bris makhn iz nit azoy shver, es kost nor a sakh gelt.

It's not very hard to make a bris, it just costs a lot in the end.

> **Bris makhn** – to perform the ritual circumcision – is also used to mean baby-making. (eds.)

Tate, mame, bobe, zeyde, kusht in tokhes unz beyde.

Daddy, mommy, grandpa, granny; kiss us both on the fanny.

> So says a young couple who have gotten married against the will of their parents and other relatives. (i.b.)

Far a meydl iz alts a sod, nor koym vert zi im gevor, iz zi shoyn a vaybl.

Everything's a mystery to a girl, and just as she finds out, she's married.

"Khosn dume l'meylakh" – as di kale is kosher, iz er freylakh.

"The groom is king" – If the bride is pure, he wants to dance and sing.

Vi biter es iz dem ber on a veydl, nokh biterer iz dem khosn, ven di kale iz nit kayn meydl.

Bitter the bear with no tail to twirl, more bitter the groom, when the bride is no virgin girl.

8

א בְּרִית מַאכְבָן אִיז נִיט אַזוֹי שְׁוֶוער, עֶס קָאסְט נָאר אַ סַךְ נֶעלְד.

טַאטֶע, מַאמֶע, בָּאבֶּע, זֵיידֶע, קוּשְׁט אִין תָּחַת אוּנְז בֵּיידֶע.

בָּאבֶּע = p. baba; זֵיידֶע = p. dziad — אוֹיך זָאנְט אַ יוּנְג פָאאָר־פָאלְק, וָואס הָאט חַתוּנָה נֶעהַאט נֶעגֶען דֶעם וִוילֶן פוּן דִי עֶלְטֶערְן אוּן דִי אִיבְּרִינֶע קְרוֹבִים.

פָאר אַ מֵיידֶעל אִיז אַלְץ אַ סוֹד, נָאר קוֹים וֶוערְט זִי אִיהֶם נֶעוָואהְר, אִיז זִי שׁוֹין אַ וֵויבֶּעל.

„חָתָן דוֹמֶה לְמֶלֶךְ" — אַז דִי כַּלָה אִיז כָּשֵׁר, אִיז עֶר פְרֵיילֶעךְ.

וִוי בִּיטֶער עֶס אִיז דָעם בֶּער אָהְן אַ וֵויידֶעל, נָאךְ בִּיטֶערֶער אִיז דֶעם חָתָן, וֶוען דִי כַּלָה אִיז נִיט קֵיין מֵיידֶעל.

9

Eyner hot lib a kale mit a sakh gelt, der anderer hot lib a kale on a hemd.

Some like a bride with a lot of money, others like a bride without a stitch of clothes.

Khuts dem nadn muz a meydl (oder: a kale) nokh hobn a gutn tsad.

Besides the dowry, a girl (or: a bride) must also have a good background.

> **Tsad** (literally, side of the family) is also an acronym for **tsitslakh** (tits) and **dupe** (ass). (i.b.)

Az an oreme kale shtelt zikh tantsn, geyen di klezmer pishn!

When a poor bride gets up to dance, the musicians go out to piss!

Dos kind iz geboyrn tsu der tsayt, nor di khupe hot men tsu shpet geshtelt.

The baby was born right on time, only the wedding was too late.

> When a young wife has a baby right after the wedding. (i.b.)

10

אײנער האט ליב א כּלָה מיט א סַךְ גֶעלד, דער אַנדערער האט ליב
א כּלָה אָהן א הֶעמד.

חוּץ דֶעם נְדַן מוז א מֵיידעל (אָדֶער : א כּלָה) נָאךְ הָאבּען א גוטען צד.
דִי ר״ת פֿון צד מאכּען : צִיצֶלעךְ, דוּפֶּע. — דוּפֶּע = p. dupa

אַז אן אָרעמע כּלָה שטעלט זיךְ טאַנצען, געהָען דִי כּלֵי־זֶמֶר פֿישֶען.

דָאס קינד אין געבּוירֶען צו דער צייט. נָאר דִי חוּפָּה הָאט מען צו שפֶּעט
וֶוען א וֵויבֶּעל בֶּעקוּמט בּאַלד נָאךְ דֶער חַתוּנָה א קינד.

11

Di khupe fardekt (oder: dekt tsu) ale aveyres.

The wedding canopy covers all sins.

> That is, if a girl sinned before the wedding, after the wedding the child is attributed to her husband and is considered legitimate. (i.b.)

Po khupye, potsaluy ve dupye!

The wedding's past, kiss my ass!

> This is what the father of the bride says to his son-in-law after the wedding, when he doesn't want to pay the dowry. (i.b.)

די חופה פֿערדָרעקט (אָדער: דעקט צו) אַלע עבֿרות.

ה. ה. ווען אַ מיידעל הָאט פֿאר דער חתונה געוויזינט, ווערט עס נָאך
דער חופה צוּגעשריבּען דעם אייגענעם מאַן און דָאס קינד איז כּשֵר.

פֿא הופּיֶע. פֿאצאלוי וון דופּיֶע.

p. po chupie pocałuj w dupie. — דָאס זָאגט נָאך דער הופּה דער
שוועהר צום איידעם, אז ע׳ וויל איהם ניט פֿאַלֶק זיין דעם נַדַן.

2. WOMEN OF VIRTUE AND OTHERWISE

Bay fish un bay a meydl iz dos beste dos mitlshtik.

With fish and with a girl — the best part is the middle.

Az a meydl falt, falt zi shtendik oyf'n rikn.

When a girl falls, she always falls on her back.

Di vaybers gantse gvure shtekt in dem tokhes.

All the fight women have is in their behinds.

A lakhndik vaybl iz kitsldik.

A laughing woman is ticklish.

Az a vaybl lakht, iz a guter simen.

If a woman laughs, it's a good sign.

Az a vaybl dreyt mit'n tokhes, iz a simen az zi iz forn kitsldik.

If a woman swings her behind, it means she's ticklish up front.

בֵּיי פֿיש אוּן בֵּיי אַ מֵיידֶעל אִיז דָאס בֶּעסטֶע דָאם מִיטֶעלשְטִיק.

אַז אַ מֵיידֶעל פֿאַלט, פֿאַלט זִי שְטֶענדִיג אוֹיפֿ'ן רִיקֶען.

דִי ווַייבֶּערם נַאצֶע נְבוּרָה שְטֶעקט אִין דֶעם תָּחָת.

אַ לַאקֶענדִיג ווַייבֶּעל אִיז קִיצֶעלדִיג.

אַז אַ ווַייבֶּעל לַאכט, אִיז אַ גוּטֶער סִימָן.

אַז אַ ווַייבֶּעל דְרֶעהט מִיט'ן תָּחָת, אִיז אַ סִימָן, אַז זִי אִיז פֿאַרן קִיצֶעלדִיג.

15

Vayber haltn vos es shteyt.

Women grasp what stands.

> Grasp what stands usually means: what stands written in the bible. Here, however, it has another meaning. (i.b.)

A vaybl mit a groysn shleyer, un hot lib harte eyer.

A woman who veils her face, likes hard eggs in the right place.

A tokhes vi a dinye, tsitslekh vi di epl, un di maynse vi a floym (oder: vi a kayzerke).

An ass like a melon, tits like apples, and a you-know-what like a plum (or: like a kaiser roll).

A nekeyve vi a damb, nor in der mit, iz a seynk.

A broad built like an oak, with a knot-hole in the middle.

A yifas-toar — a fas vi a toyer un a tokhes vi a raybayzn.

Some beauty — a hole like a gate and a behind like a grating board.

> Said of a very fat and ugly woman. (i.b.)

16

װײבּער האלטען, װאס עם שטעהט.

„האלטען, װאס עם שטעהט" מײנט מען נעװעהנליך: װאס עם שטעהט געשריבּען אין
דער תּורה. דא האט עם אבּער אן אנדערע טײטש.

א װײבּעל מיט א נרױסען שלײער, און האט ליב דאַרטע אײער.

א תּחת װי א דיננע, צוצלעך װי די עפּעל, און די מעשׂה װי א פּלױם

(אָדער: װי א קינדערקע.)

p. kajzerka = קײזערקע; p. dynia = דיננע

א נקבה װי א דאָמבּ, נאר אין דער מיטם איז א סאָנק.

p. sęk = סענק; p. dąb = דאָמבּ

א יפת-תּאַר — א פּאס װי א טױער און א תּחת װי א רײבּאײזען.
פֿון זעהר א דיקער און מיאוסער נקבה.

Bay ir in mitn, ken men araynforn mit a shlitn.

Through her hole, it's been said, you can drive with a sled.

Az men makht tsu di lodn, iz a mise moyd oykh a flodn.

With the shutters shut, even an ugly girl's a honey pot.

An eyshes-ish iz vi maton b'seyser.

A married women is like giving to charity.

> That is, you never know how much it's costing you. (i.b.)

A hur muz men foroys betsoln.

With a whore, you've got to pay first.

A kurve git nit oyf kredit, vorum ir gesheft iz nor oyf a minit.

A whore doesn't give on credit, because her business only lasts a minute.

A hur git on a shir, nor bay itlikher mol zogt zi: "Betsol".

A whore puts out forever, but each time around she says: "Pay."

בֵּיי אִיהר אִין מִיטְעַן, קָען מָען אַרַיינְפָאהְרֶען מִיט אַ שְׁלִיטֶען.

אַז מֶען מַאכְט צוּ דִי לָאדֶען, אִיז אַ מִיאוּסֶ׳ע מוֹיד אוֹיךְ אַ פְלָאדֶען.

אַן אֵשֶׁת־אִישׁ אִיז וִי אַ מַתָּן בְּסֵתֶר.
ד. ה. מֶען וַייסְט נִיט, וָואס מֶען לֶעבְּט אִין אִיהר אַרַיין.

אַ הוּר מוּז מֶען פָארוּם בֶּעצָאהְלֶען.

אַ קוּרְוֶוע גִיט נִיט אוֹיף אַ קְרֶעדִיט, וָוארוּם אִיהר גֶעשֶׁעפְט אִיז נָאר אוֹיף אַ מִינוּט.
קוּרְוֶוע = p. kurwa

אַ הוּר נִיט אָהָן אַ שִׁיעוּר, נָאר בֵּיי אִיטְלִיכָען מָאל זָאנְט ד׳: בֶּעצָאהְל.

19

A kurve far eynem, iz a kurve far ale.

A whore for one is a whore for all.

A hur iz vi a tinthorn.

A whore is like an inkwell.

That is, everyone can dip his pen. (i.b.)

Shpay a hur in ponim arayn, zogt zi, es regnt.

Spit in a whore's face, she'll say it's raining.

B'shas hadkhak iz a krume nekeyve oykh gut – abi zi ligt nor glaykh.

When you're horny, even a gimpy whore will do - as long as she lies straight.

Az dos vayb iz a hur, vert der man a gevir.

If the wife is a whore, the husband becomes a rich man.

Di mume Khaye, tso za dva groshi dupe daye.

My aunt Tess, for two cents she'll get on her ass.

A Polish saying. (eds.)

א קוּרְוָע פַּאר אֵיינֶעם, אִיז אַ קוּרְוָוע פַּאר אַלֶע.

א הוּר אִיז ווי אַ טִינְטְהָארְן.
ד. ה. אִיטְלִיכֶער מֶען דִי פַּען אַרַיינְשְׁטֶעקֶען.

שְׁפַּיי אַ הוּר אִין פָּנִים אַרַיין, זָאגְט זִי, עֶס רֶעגֶענְט.

בִּשְׁעַת הַדְּחַק אִיז אַ קְרוּמֶע נְקֵבָה אוּיךְ נוּט – אַבִּי זִי לִינְט נָאר גְלַייךְ.
אַבִּי = p. aby

אַז דָאם ווַייב אִיז אַ הוּר, ווֶערְט דֶער מַאן אַ גְבִיר.

דִי מוּהְמֶע חַיָה, צָא זַא דְווַא גְרָאשִׁי דוּפֶּע דַאיֶע.
p. co za dwa groszy dupę daje.

21

Khane, khane, loz dir makhn fun forn a kane.

Hanna, Hanna, let's give your frontside an enema.

Raytsi, az men trent zi, shrayt zi.

Tina, when you ream her, is a screamer.

Aza yor oyf mir vi men ligt oyf ir.

Just give me as good a time as they have on her.

Di kekhn ken aleyn makhn a kugl, ober a kind lost zi zikh makhn fun dem balebos.

The cook can make a pudding by herself, but she lets the boss make her a baby.

Az di rebitsin heyst zikh dreyen, tor zi der belfer nit deragzenen.

When the rabbi's wife is looking around, she'd better stay on the assistant's good side.

Zay nit mayn man, un shtip mir nit di hant in buzem arayn — un tifer, avade nit.

Don't be my man, and don't stick your hand into my bosom — and certainly not any further.

> So says a young wife to a fellow who wants to get too fresh with her. (i.b.)

22

חַנָה, חַנָה, לָאז דיר מַאכֶן פֿון פָֿאָרְן אַ קַאנֶע!

קַאנֶע = p. kanka

בֵּייצִי, אַז מֶען טרֶעגְט זי, שְׁרֵייט זי.

אַזַא יָאהְר אוֹיף מיר, ווי מֶען ליגְט אוֹיף איהְר.

די קֶעכִין קֶען אַלֵיין מַאכֶן אַ קוּגֶעל, אָבֶער אַ.קינְד לָאזְט זי זיך מַאכֶן פֿון דֶעם בַּעל־בָּית.

אַז די רַבִּיצִין הֵייכְט זיך דְרַעהֶען, מָאר זי דֶער בַּעלפַֿער ניט דֶערדַאנְזֶענַען.

זֵיי ניט מֵיין מַאן, אוּן שְׁטֵיט מיר ניט די הַאנְד אין בּוּזֶעם אַרֵיין – אוּן טיפַֿער, אַדְרַאי ניט.
אַזוֹי זָאגְט אַ ווֵייבֶּעל צוּ־נַ'א מַאנְסְפַּעָרְשׁוֹין, וָואָס עֶר ווִיל זִיט איהְר צוּ־פִֿיל קַאטָאווֶעס טְרֵייבֶּען.

23

3. MEN ABOUT TOWN

Der nogid pisht nit mit boyml, un kakt nit mit grivn.

A rich man doesn't piss olive oil and doesn't crap **grivn**.

> **Grivn** is a delicacy made from well-browned roasted bits of goose or chicken skin. (eds.)

A meyukhes, kusht in tokhes.

Your upper class, kiss my ass.

> There isn't much respect for family in the world these days. (i.b.)

An erlikher yid! In der fri (oder: tsu shakhres) kusht er tsitsis, bay nakht (oder: nokh mayriv) kusht er tsitskes.

An honest man! In the morning (or: at morning prayers) he kisses his prayer shawl, at night (or: after evening prayers) he kisses tits and all.

Dem erlikhstn yidn tor men nit getroyen a baytl mit gelt tsu-kopns un a meydl tsu-fusns, vorum der baytl vet vern leydig un dos meydl ful.

Even the most honest man should not be trusted with a purse at the head of his bed and a girl at the foot; the purse will wind up empty and the girl full.

דער נאָיד פֿישט ניט מיט בוימעל, און קאַקט ניט מיט גרינען.

א מיוחס. קושט אין תָּחָת.
די באַינטינע וועלט האָט ניט קיין נדוישען בעד־אַרץ פֿאַר א מיוחס.

אן אָהרליכער ייד! אין דער פֿריה (אָדער: צו שַחֲרִית) קושט ער ציצת, בײַ נאַכט
(אָדער: נאָך מַעֲרִיב) קושט ער ציצקעם.

דעם עהרליכסטען יודען טאָר מען ניט נעטרויען א ביטעל מיט געלד צוקאאפֿענם און א מיידעל צוּפֿאסענם. וואָרום דער ביטעל וועט ווערען לעדיג און דאָס מיידעל פֿול.

Er geyt arum mit a kaziyone tokhes.

He goes around with an innocent ass.

> In Russia this is said of someone who did some
> sinning and is afraid of being punished. (i.b.)

*Er dreyt zikh arum vi a forts in bod (oder. . .in a lamtern;
oder. . .in rosl).*

He wanders around like a fart in the bathtub (or. . .in a
lantern; or. . .in a pickle barrel).

Er klebt zikh tsu, vi dos hemd tsum tokhes.

He sticks to you, like your shirt to your butt.

> About a bore who can't be gotten rid of. (i.b.)

Shmuel shmok, in eyn shukh, in eyn zok!

Sammy cock, in one shoe, in one sock!

> Said about a great bungler. (i.b.)

Zayn gantser koyekh geyt arayn inem vaybershn tokhes.

All his energy goes into his wife's behind.

Es shteyt bay im vi bay an ogyer.

He's got one like a stallion's.

עֶר נֶעהְט אַרוּם מִיט אַ קאָזיאַנֶע תַּחַת.

קאָזיאָנֶע = r. казённый — אִין רוּסלאַנד זאָגְט מֶען דאָס פֿוּן אֵיינֶעם, וואָס
עֶר האָט עֶפֶּעס פֿאַרזִינדיגְט אוּן האָט מוֹרָא, מֶען זאָל אִיהְם נִיט בַּעשְׁטראָפֿען.

עֶר דְרֶעהְט זִיך אַרוּם ווִי אַ פֿאָרץ אִין בָּאד (אָדֶער:... אִין אַ לאַמְטֶערְן;
אָדֶער... אִין ראָסֶעל.)
ראָסֶעל = p. rosół.

עֶר קלֶעבְּט זִיך צוּ ווִי דאָס הֶעמְד צוּם תַּחַת.
פֿוּן אַ לעסטיגען מֶענְשֶׁען, וואָס מֶען קֶען זִיך פֿוּן אִיהְם נִיט אָפְּטשֶׁעפֶּען.

שְׁמוּאֵל שְׁמאַק, אִין אֵיין שׁוּה, אִין אֵיין זאַק!
פֿוּן אַ גְרוֹיסֶען לאַ־יצְלָח.

זַיין גאַנְצֶער כֹּחַ נֶעהְט אַרַיין אִינְ'ם ווייבֶּערשֶׁען תַּחַת.

עֶס שְׁטֶעהְט בַּיי אִיהְם ווִי בַּיי אַן אָניֶער.
אָניֶער = p. ogier

Er hot in di hoyzn a yarid.

He's got an uproar in his pants.

>That is: He is ill with syphilis. (i.b.)

Er hot bekumen Boaz's shrek.

He got Boaz's fright.

>When one is startled on seeing a pretty piece; the same as Boaz, poor thing, was startled when he found Ruth in bed with him (". . .and he was startled by the woman and turned himself"; Ruth: 3.8) (i.b.)

Far vos iz a melamed a shvants? Vayl er geyt beyn regl l'regl.

Why is a tutor a prick? Because he lives between fetes.

>The original pun is on "regl" as foot and "regl" as holiday. The malamed, usually poor, depended on holiday meals for sustenance. (eds.)

Rebe, di dinst trogt! "Vos geyt es mikh on?" — Men zogt, es iz fun aykh — "Vos'zshe geyt es dikh on?"

Rabbi, the servant girl's pregnant! "So what's it to me?" — They say it's yours. — "So what's it to you?"

עֶר הָאט אִין דִי הוֹזְן אַ יָרִיד.

ד. ה. עֶר אִיז קְרַאנְק אוֹיף סִיפִֿילִיס.

עֶר הָאט בַּעקוּמֶען בֶּעזֶעם שְׁרֶעק.

וֶוען אַיינֶער הֶירְשְׁצֶעקְט זִיךְ קְלָאפֶּערְשְׁט, אוּ עֶר דָערְזֶעהְט אַ שִׁיינֶע נְקֵבָה, אוֹי וֶו בַּעֹ
הָאט זִיךְ נֶעבִּיךְ דָערְשְׁרָאקֶען, אוּ עֶר הָאט רוּת נֶעטָֿונֶען בַּיי זִיךְ אִין בֶּעטְט (...וַיֶּחֱרַד
הָאִישׁ וַיִּלָּפֵֿת.) רוּת נ. ה.

פַֿאר וָואם אִיז אַ מְלַמֵד אַ שְׁוַואנְק ? – וַויל עֶר נֶעהְט בֵּין רֶגֶל לְרֶגֶל.

וָוארְטְשְׁפִּיל צְוִוישֶׁען „רֶגֶל“ = יוֹם-טוֹב אוּן „רֶגֶל“ = פֿוּם.

רֶבִּי, דִי דִינְסְט טְרָאנְט ! – „וָואם נֶעהְט עֶם מִיךְ אָן ?“ – מֶען זָאנְט, עֶם
אִיז פֿון אַיְיךְ. – „וָואסְדֶושֶׁע נֶעהְט עֶם דִיךְ אָן ?“

4. THE MARRIAGE BED

Di kale halt zikh tsu di oygn in der khupe-nakht, ober zi kukt durkh di finger.

The bride hides her eyes on the wedding night, but she peeks through her fingers.

Di kale shemt zikh, ober hanoye hot zi fort.

The bride is bashful, but she enjoys it all the same.

A khupe shtelt men, un dos porfolk baleygt men.

At a wedding, you put the canopy up and the couple to bed.

Nokh der khupe leygt men khosn-kale oyf eyn kupe (nont tsu der dupe).

After the wedding, pile the bride and groom on the bedding (close enough for petting).

Di khupe-nakht iz afile in vinter tsu kleyn.

Even in winter, the wedding night is too short.

Nor tsulib der ershter nakht aleyn, hot men nit khasene.

For the first night alone is no reason to get married.

די כַּלָה הַאלְט זִיךְ צוּ דִי אוֹיגָן אִין דֶער חוּפָּה־נַאכְט, אָבֶּער זִי קוּקְט דוּרְךְ דִי פֿינגֶער.

די כַּלָה שֶׁעמְט זִיךְ, אָבֶּער הַנָאָה הָאט זִי פֿאָרְט.

אַ חוּפָּה שְׁטֶעלְט מֶען, אוֹן דָאם פֿאָר־פֿאָלְק בֶּעלֶעגְט מֶען.

נָאךְ דֶער חוּפָּה, לֶענְט מֶען חָתָן־כַּלָה אוֹיף אַיין קוּפֶּע (נָאהֶענְט צוּ דֶער דוּפֶּע.)
קוּפֶּע = p. kupa ; דוּפֶּע = p. dupa

די חוּפָּה־נַאכְט אִיז אֲפֿילוּ אִין ווינְטֶער צוּ קְלַיין.

נָאר צוּ־ליב דֶער עֶרְשְׁטֶער נַאכְט אַלֵיין, הָאט מֶען ניט חַתוּנָה.

31

Nit fil getrakht, un in der ershter nakht a kind gemakht.

Didn't give it much thought, and out of the first night, a baby brought.

> A regular genius of a girl — may no evil befall her. (i.b.)

A kush a vaybl iz a zadatek.

Kissing a young wife is like making a down-payment.

A yung vaybl hot lib a grobe kishke mit harte eyer.

A young wife likes thick sausage with hard eggs.

A genite kale leygt zikh aleyn oyf'n rikn.

An experienced bride gets right on her back.

Mit a yung vaybl iz gut tsu shpiln in loteriye, — zi iz tomid a gevinerin.

It's good to play dice with a young wife — she always comes.

> "Gevinerin" means both "winner" and "a woman lying in." (eds.)

ניט פֿיל נֶעטראַכט, און אין דֶער עֶרשטֶער נאַכט נֶעכט אַ קינד נֶעמאַכט.
סאָק ־אַיו ־גוֹדהאָה אַ בְּנָה.

א קוֹש אַ וַויבֶּעל איז אַ זַאדאָטעק.

זַאדאָטֶעק = p. zadatek

א יונג ווייבֶּעל האָט ליב אַ גראָבֶּע קישקֶע מיט האַרטֶע אייער.
קישקֶע = p. kiszka — פֶּערֶל.

א נֶעניטֶע כַּלָה לֶעגט זיך אַליין אויפֿן ריקֶען.

מיט א יונג ווייבֶּעל איז נוט צו שפֿילֶען אין לאָטֶערֶיע – זי איז תָמִיד
א נֶעווינֶערין.

33

A yidish vaybl muz ophitn ir MITOH.

A Jewish wife must take care of her bed.

> The constituents of the acronym MITOH are "M'likho" (salting of meat), "T'vilo" (the ritual bath), and "Hadloko" (lighting the Sabbath candles). the three injunctions of Jewish womanhood. But here is meant simply "mito," the bed, it should not become unclean. (i.b.)

A vayb toyg nor in bet arayn.

A wife's place is in bed.

A ful bet mit vayb (oder: mit fleysh).

A bed full of wife (or: of meat).

> Said of a very fat woman. (i.b.)

Az men shloft mit'n vayb, shtelt men der velt dem tokhes aroys.

When you sleep with your wife, you show your behind to the world.

> What this refers to is the position of the man during intercourse. (i.b.)

Peysakh iz itlikher yid meylekh iber a (vaybershn) tokhes.

At Passover every man is a king — over a (wifely) behind.

א יודיש ווײבּעל מוז אָבּהיטען איהר מטָה.

די ר"ת פֿון מטָה מאַכּען: מליחָה, טְבִילָה, הַדְלָקָה, די דרײַ מצות, וואָס אַ יודינע מוז אָבּהיטען, דאָ מײנט מען אָבּער פּשוט מטָה, דאָס בּעטט, עס זאָל ניט טמא ווערען.

א ווײב טוט נאָר אין בּעטט אַרײַן.

א פֿול בּעטט מיט ווײב (אָדער: ...מיט פֿלײש.)

פֿון זעהר א דיקער נקבֿה.

או מען שלאָפֿט מיטן ווײב. שטעלט מען דאָך ווער וועלט דעם תָחת אַרוים.

מען דענקט זיך דערבּײַ די פֿאָזיצע פֿונם מאן בּשַעת תשמיש.

פּסח איז איטליכּער יוד א מלך איבּער א (ווײבּערשען) תָחת.

Mit an eygn vayb, ven ikh vil, mit a fremd vayb, ven zi vil.

With my own wife when I want; with someone else's wife, when she wants.

An eygn vayb hot men tomid, a fremd vayb iz a marokhe.

Your own wife can always have, someone else's wife is a bit of good luck.

An eygn vayb iz gut bay nakht, a fremd vayb muz men bay tog oykh banutsn.

Your own wife is good at night; someone else's wife − in the daytime too.

Az dos vayb geyt in mikve arayn, kukt der man fun'm fenster aroys.

When the wife goes to the bath house, the husband stands at the window.

> That is: He watches impatiently for her to come out. (i.b.)

> The wife must be ritually cleansed in the bathhouse (**mikve**) following her period before she can again have realtions with her husband. (eds.)

Az di tukerin shrayt: kosher, kosher! meg zikh der man oyf ir farlozn (oder:. . .iz es mistome vi'erne).

When the bathhouse attendant shouts: Kosher, Kosher! the husband can depend on it (or. . .it is probably true).

מיט אן אייגען ווייב, וועז איך וויל, מיט א פֿרעמד ווייב, וועז זי וויל.

אן אייגען ווייב האט מעז תָּמִיד, א פֿרעמד ווייב איז א מַעֲרָכָה.

אן אייגען ווייב איז נוט ביי נאכט, א פֿרעמד ווייב מוז מעז ביי מאז אויך בענוצעז.

אז דאָס ווייב געהט אין מִקְוֶה אַרײַן, קוקט דער מאן פֿון'ם פֿענסטער אַרוים.
ד. ה. ער קוקט אויף איהר אַרוים מיט אומגעדולד.

אז די טוקערין שרײַט: כּשר כּשר! מעז זיך דער מאן אויף איהר פֿערלאָזעז. (אדער: ... איז עם מסתּמא ווערנע.)
ווערנע = r. вѣрно

Az dos vayb hot di vest, hot der man shlekhte kest.

When the wife has the curse, the husband's keep is at its worst.

Az dos vayb iz a nide, hot der man a bide.

When the wife is bloody, the man feels cruddy.

> **Nido** is the menstrual period; **bide** (from the Polish **bieda**) means the misery of a poor soul, a wretch. (eds.)

Az dos vayb git nit, meg zikh der man afile ofy'n kop shteln.

When the wife's not giving any, the husband might as well stand on his head.

Az dos vayb hot moyre zi zol nit m'ubres vern, ret zi dem man ayn as zi zeygt bay tog dos kind.

If the wife is afraid of getting pregnant, she lets her husband think she's still nursing.

> Intercourse with nursing mothers is forbidden by Jewish law. (eds.)

Az dos vayb iz broyges, leyent zi op krishma un dreyt zikh um tzum man mit'n tokhes.

When the wife is angry, she says her prayers, and turns her behind to her husband.

38

אז דאָס װײב האָט די װעסט, האָט דער מאַן דער שלעכטע קעסט.

אז דאָס װײב איז אַ נדה, האָט דער מאַן אַ בידע.

בידע = bieda

אז דאָס װײב ניט ניט, מען זיך דער מאַן אַפֿילו אויפֿן קאָפּ שטעלן.

אז דאָס װײב האָט מוֹרא זי זאָל ניט מעוּבֶּרֶת װערען, רעדט זי דעם מאַן אײַן, אז זי זײַנט בײַ טאָג דאָס קינד.

אז דאָס װײב איז ברוֹגֶז, לײענט זי אָב קריאת־שמע און דרעהט זיך אום צום מאַן מיטן תָּחַת.

39

Az der man iz foyl aroyftsukrikhn, muz dos vayb arunterkrikhn.

If the husband doesn't feel like climbing on top, the wife has to crawl underneath.

Ven der rov hot afile oyfn petsl a kretsl, — di rebitsn iz es fort mekabl b'havo.

Even when the Rabbi has a chancre on his cock, his wife takes it with love.

Zikh aleyn, vi men vil, ober a vayb a kind muz men makhn.

Suit yourself if it's for you — but for a wife you have to make a baby.

> Actually the saying is to "make some clothes." Here, however, it simply means "make a baby for your wife." (i.b.)

Men traybt mit a vaybl azoy katoves, biz es kumt aroys a kleyner emes.

You fool around and fool around with a wife until out comes a little seriousness.

Vos erger di kest, vos mer makht men kinder.

The worse things are, the more babies.

> Equivalent English saying: "The rich get richer and the poor get children." (eds.)

אז דער מאַן איז פֿויל אַרויפֿצוקריכן, מוז דאָס װײַב אַרונטערקריכן.

װען דער רב האָט אַפֿילו אויפֿ'ם פֿעצעל אַ קרעצעל, – די רביצין איז עס פֿאַרט מקבל באַהבֿה.

זיך אַלײן, װי מען װיל, אָבער אַ װײַב אַ קינד מוז מען מאַכן.
אײנעטליך זאָל עס הײסן: "קלײידער" מאַכן, דאָ מײנט מען אָבער פּשוט: דעם װײַב אַ קינד מאַכן.

מען טרײַבט מיט אַ װײַבעל אַזוי לאַנג קאַטאָװעס, ביז עס קומט אַרוים אַ קלײנער אמת.

װאָס ערגער די קעסט, װאָס מעהר מאַכט מען קינדער.

41

A m'uberes vaybl ken shoyn m'ubreser nit vern — rayb-zhe Motye, vayter.

A pregnant wife can't get any pregnanter — grind away, Motye.

Az der tsar fun'm trogen iz yo azoy groys, vu nemen zikh azoy fil amen?

If pregnancy is so much grief, why are there so many nursemaids?

Tsum trogn muzn zayn tsvey, tsum hobn iz genug eyne aleyn.

To carry takes two, to have — one alone will do.

Vos shverer a vaybl geyt tsu kind, vos mer hot zi hanoyeh gehat baym makhn.

The harder the baby comes out, the more fun she had making it.

א מְעוּבֶּרֶת וַוייבֶּעל קֶען שוין מְעוּבֶּרֶתֶער ניט וֶוערֶען – רייב־זשֶע, מָאטֶיע, וַוייטֶער.

אַז דָער צַער פֿון'ם טְרָאנְגֶען איז יָא אַזוי גְרוים, ווַאו נֶעמֶען זיך אַזוי פֿיר אַמֶען?

צום טְרָאגֶען מוּז'ן זיין צְוֶוייי, צום הָאבֶּען איז גֶענוּג איינֶע אַליין.

וָואס שְוֶוטְרֶער אַ ווייבֶּעל גֶעהְט צוּ־קִינְד, וָואס מֶעהְר הָאט וִי הֲנָאָה גֶעהַאט ביים מַאכֶּן.

5. THE CRUX OF THE MATTER

Lost zikh friyer a kush gebn a meydl, meg men ir shpeter oyfheyben dos kleydl.

If a girl lets you give her a kiss and a press, later she'll let you pick up her dress.

Baym ershtn mol shrayt a meydl "oy, oy, oy!" Baym tsveytn mol lakht zi "kha, kha, kha."

The first time a girl cries "ooh, ooh, ooh!" The second time she laughs "ha, ha, ha!"

Tsu der shpits brust, hot itlikhn a gelust.

Who doesn't lust for the tip of the bust?

    One means here, of course, the womanly bust. (i.b.)

Eyder du krikhst oyf a meydl, greyt friyer on dem veydl.

Prepare your dick before you do your trick.

לָאזְט זִיךְ פְרִיהָער אַ קוּש נָעבָּען אַ מֵיידֶעל. מָען מָען אִיהַר שְפֶּעטָער
אוֹיפָּהָעבֶּען דָאס קְלֵיידֶעל.

בֵּיים עָרְשְׁטָען מָאל שְרַיים אַ מֵיידָעל „אוֹי, אוֹי, אוֹי!" – בֵּיים צְוַויטָען
מָאל לַאכְט זִי „חַא, חַא, חַא!"

צוּ דָער שְׁפִּיץ בְּרוּסְט,הָאט אִיטְלִיכָער אַ גָעלוּסְט.
מָען מֵיינְט דָא אַדְרַאי דִי טַייפֶערְשֶׁע בְּרוּסְט.

אֵיידֶער דוּ קְרִיקְסְט אוֹיךְ אַ מֵיידָעל, גְרֵייט פְרִיהָער אָן דֶעם וַוִידֶעל.

45

Hob ikh a shikse, hob ikh kayn ort nit, hob ikh an ort, hob ikh kayn shikse nit, hob ikh beyde, vil der kleyner nit shteyn.

If I have a **shiksa**, then I have no place, if I have a place, then I have no **shiksa**, if I have both, then the little one won't stand.

    A **shiksa** is a Gentile girl. (eds.)

Ahin un aher, un in der mit a lokh — vozhe vartstu nokh? — Makh a shtokh!

Back and forth and in the middle a hole — What are you waiting for? — Stick in your pole.

Eyn mol fun forn, un eyn mol fun hintn, iz po kozatske (oder: hot a tam k'tsapikhis bidvash).

Once from the front and once from behind is more fun than a polka (or: is as tasty as a honey cake).

Fun forn ken ikh dir, mayn man, nit veyrn, ober dem tokhes — kadokhes.

The front, my man, is yours by right, but the behind — burn all night.

Gots vunder, a puts makht kinder!

Wonder of God, children come from a rod!

46

הָאב איך אַ שׁיקסע, הָאב איך אַ קײן אָרֶט ניט, הָאב איך אָן אָרֶט,
הָאב איך קײן שׁיקסע ניט, הָאב איך בײדע, װיל דֶער קלײנֶער ניט
שׁטֶעהָען.

אַהין און אַהֶער, און אין דֶער מיטט אַ לָאך – װָאס־זשֶׁע װַארטֶסט דו
נָאך ? – מַאך אַ שׁטָאך !

אײן מָאל פון פָארן, און אײן מָאל פון הינטֶן איז פָא קָאזַאצקֶע (אָדֶר:
הָאט אַ טַעם כְּצַפִיחִית בִּדְבָשׁ.)
פָא קָאזַאצקֶע = p. po kozacku

פון פָארן קֶען איך דיר, מײן מאן, ניט קֶעהָרֶן אָבֶער דֶעם תָּחַת – קַדָחַת !

נָאטם װאונדֶער, אַ פָא מאכט קונֶדֶר !

47

Der kleyner iz on beyner, un ale beyner kumen fun im aroys.

The little one has no bones, but all bones come from him.

Der grester ganef iz der kleyner. durkh dem klenstn lekhl krikht er arayn.

The little one is the greatest thief; he sneaks in through the smallest hole.

Der kleyner hot nor eyn oyg, un treft fort in der finster.

The little one has only one eye, but in the dark he finds his mark.

Vi azoy treft der blinder tsum vayb in bet arayn? – Der kleyner firt im.

How does a blind man find his way to his wife's bed? – The little one leads him.

> Ordinarily a blind man lets himself be led around by a small boy (the little one). Here, however, by "the little one" is meant the "evil urge." (i.b.)
> We don't think so. (eds.)

Der kleyner shoykelt mitn kop. un di kleyne makht zikh nit visndik.

The little one, he nods his head, and the little one, she pretends not to understand.

דער קלֵיינֶער איז אָהן בֵּיינֶער, און אַלֶע בֵּיינֶער קומֶען פון איהם אַרוים.

דער גרֶעסטֶער גַנֵב איז דער קלֵיינֶער, דורך דֶעם קלֵיינסטֶען לֶעכֶעל קריכט ער אַרַיין.

דער קלֵיינֶער האָט נאָר אֵיין אויג, און טרֶעפֶּט פָּאַרט אין דֶער פֿינסטֶער.

ווי אַזוי טרֶעפֶּט דֶער בּלינדֶער צום וַיֵיב אין בֶּעטֶט אַריין? – דֶער קלֵיינֶער פֿיהרט איהם.
נֶעטֶעהנליך לאָזֶט זיך אַ בּלינדֶער אַרויספֿיהרֶען פֿון אַ קלֵיין יונֶגֶעל (דֶער קלֵיינֶער). דאָ מֵיינֶט מֶען אָבֶּער אונטֶער דֶעם קלֵיינֶער דֶעם צַו־הָרָע, וואָס פֿיהרט דֶעם בּלינדֶען דֶעם וֶועג צום ווֵיב.

דֶער קלֵיינֶער שוֵיקֶעלט מִיטְן קאָפּ, און די קלֵיינֶע מאַכט זיך ניט ווסֶענדיג.

49

Az der kleyner vil nit shteyn leygt men im in der gemore arayn.

When the little one won't stand, you put him in the Talmud.

> Because they say everything stands [written] in the Talmud. (i.b.)

Az der kleyner vil nit shteyn, muz men zikh mitn finger bageyn.

If the little one won't stand, you have to do it all by hand.

Vey iz dem man, ven der kleyner vil nit shteyn un dos vayb muz zikh mitn finger bageyn.

Woe to the man when his tool refuses action, and his wife must use a finger, to get her satisfaction.

Az der mentsh iz umetik lost der kleyner oykh arop dem kop.

When a man is sad, the little one also hangs his head.

A shtumpik meser, un trent fort dem vaybershn pelts.

A dull knife, but it can still part a woman's furpiece.

50

אז דער קלײנער װיל ניט שטעהן, לעגט מען אים אין דער גמרא אַרײן.
װײל מען זאָגט, אין דער גמרא שטעהט אַלעם.

אז דער קלײנער װיל ניט שטעהן, מוז מען זיך מיטן פֿינגער בעטהען.

װעה איז דעם מאן, װען דער קלײנער װיל ניט שטעהן און דאָם
װײב מוז זיך מיטן פֿינגער בעטהען.

אז דער מענש איז אומגוטהיג, לאָזט דער קלײנער אויך אַראָב דעם קאָפ.

א שטומפֿיג מעסער, און טרענט פֿאָרט דעם װײבערשען פֿעלק.

51

Kurts un dik, fun eyn shtik, un gut in gatonek.

Thick and short, not one wart, and of the best sort.

> About the large object of a circumcision ceremony.
> (i.b.)

Nit do kayn geshmakers, vi a groyser puts un a kleyn futs.

There is no finer art, then a large cock and a small fart.

A puts vi a drang, a pireg vi a flodn.

A cock like a pole, a snatch like a honey pot.

Dray mol noz, iz eyn mol dos.

Three times the nose, equals one times the hose.

> It is said that you can tell the size of someone's
> member by the size of his nose. (i.b.)

Vi bay a nekeyve dos moyl iz, azoy iz bay ir tsvishn di fis.

The way a woman's mouth is, that's the way it is between
her legs.

> Just as you can tell (the size of) a man from his nose,
> so you can tell from a woman's mouth and lips how
> sensual she is. (i.b.)

Beser a fleyshiker pireg, eyder a milekhdiker varenik.

Give me a meat pie rather than a cheese bun, any day.

קורץ און דיק פֿון איין שטיק, און גוט און נאַטאַנעק.

נאַטאַנעק = p. gatunek – פֿון אַ גרויסען בְּרִית־קֹדֶש.

ניט דאָ קיין געשמאַקערס, ווי אַ גרויסער פֿאַן און אַ קלײנע פֿאַן.

אַ פֿאַן ווי אַ דראָנג, אַ פֿירען ווי אַ פֿלאַדען.

דראָנג = p. drąg ; פֿירען = r. пирогъ

דרײַ מאָל נאָ, איז איין מאָל דאָס.

מען זאָגט, אַז מען דערקענט אַן דער נאָ די גרעס פֿון אַ ...

ווי בײַ אַ נְקֵבָה דאָס מויל איז, אוו איז בײַ איהר צְווישען די פֿים.

אַדי ווי מען דערקענט בײַ אַ זָכָר אַן דָער נאָ, אַזוי דערקענט מען בײַ אַ נְקֵבָה אַן דעם
מויל און אַן די ליפֿען, צי די האָט אַ גרויסען עֶרוּת־הָרַע.

בֶּעסער אַ פֿלײשינער פֿירען, אײדער אַ מילכדינער וואַרעניק.

פֿירען = r. пирогъ ; וואַרעניק = r. вареникъ

53

A pireg iz nit kayn krepl, er vert keyn mol nit farmiest.

Meat pie isn't like pastry — you never get tired of it.

> Because another proverb says: you can get tired of pastry too. (i.b.)

A varenik iz gut mit shvartse berlekh, a pireg iz gut mit shvartse herlekh.

A fruit pie is good filled with blackberries; a meat pie is good when it's black and hairy.

Der pelts unter dem vaybershn boykh iz dos tayerste futerl.

The pelt under a woman's belly is the world's most expensive furpiece.

Itlikhes tepl gefint zikh zayn shtertsl, itlikhes petsl gefint zikh zayn lekhl.

Every pot fins its own lid, every pole finds its own hole.

Fun a kush a vaybl vert nit kayn lokh, ober men iz neynter tsun im.

One kiss doesn't get you a hole, but it brings you closer to it.

Kush in morsh arayn, vest du hobn a ledern baytele.

Kiss what's nasty, and your bag will turn to leather.

א פֿירָען איז ניט קיין קְרָעפּפֿעל, עֶר וֶוערט קיין מָאל ניט פֿעֶר׳מָיאוסְ׳ט.

ווייל אַן אַנדֶער שְפֿריכְוָזָארְט זָאנְט: קרָעפּפֿליך וֶוערען אויך פֿעֶר׳מָיאוסְ׳ט.

אַ וַזארֶעניק איז נוט מִיט שָוַוארְצֶע בָּעֶרְלָעך; אַ פֿירָען איז נוט מִיט שָוַוארְצֶע הָעֶרְלָעך.

וַזארֶעניק = г. пирогъ ; פֿירָען = г. вареникъ

דָעֶר פֿעֶלְץ אונטֶער דָעם ווייבֶּערְשָעֶן בייך איז דָאס מְהַיֶעֶרְסְטֶע פֿוטֶערְעֶל.

אִיטְליכֶם מֶעפּפֿעל נֶעפּינְט זיך זיין שְטֶערְצֶעל, אִיטְליכֶם פֿעצֶעל נֶעפּינְט זיך זיין לָעכֶעל.

פֿון אַ קושׁ אַ ווייבֶּעל וֶזערט ניט קיין לָאך, אָבֶּער מֶען איז נֶעהֶענְטֶער צונ׳אִיהֶם.

קושׁ אִין מָארְשׁ אַריין, וֶזעסְט דו הָאבֶּען אַ לָעדֶעֶרֶען בייטֶעלֶע.

55

In di zumer-khedoshim zol men tsuru lozn di noshim.

In the summer-months it's best to let the women have a rest.

A shmukler meg dreyen zayn eygene shnur, ober fremde zol er lozn tsu-ru.

A tailor can thread his own needle, but others' he should leave alone.

> Originally a play on the word **shnur**, meaning daughter-in-law, and ,**shnur**, meaning thread: what a **shmukler** (lacemaker) plays with. (i.b.)

Mikhl un rekhl shpiln zikh beyde in petsl-lekhl.

Rachel and Dick play hole and stick.

Zi iz im mefarnes un er iz zi mezane.

She feeds him and he provides for her.

> Wordplay on **hazon v'mefarnes** meaning food and nourishment. (i.b.)

Ale "tsu" zenen shlekht — nor "rik dikh tsu" iz gut.

All "to's" are curses — but "come to me" is good.

> For example, "To the devil. . .", "To hell with you . . .", etc. (eds.); [but] when you tell a woman to slide over next to you. . . (i.b.)

אין די זומער-חֳדָשִים, זָאל מֶען צו־דוה לָאזֶען די נָשִים.

א שְמוּקלֶער מֶען דְרֶעהֶען זַיין אֵיינֶענֶע שָנוּר, אָבֶער פֿרֶעמדֶע זָאל עֶר לָאזֶען צו־דוה.
שְמוּקלֶער = p. szmuklerz — וָאירטשפֿיל צוויִישֶען דֶעם וָואירט שָנוּר = שְווינֶער-סאקטֶער אין דֶער שָנוּר, וָואס דֶער שְמוּקלֶער מאכֿט.

מִיכֶעל אוּן רֶעחֶעל שְפֿילֶען זִיך בֵּיידֶע אין פֶעצֶעל-לֶעבֶעל.

זִי אִיז אִיהֶם מְפֿרֶנֶס, אוּן עֶר אִיז זִי מְזַנֶה.
וָואירטשפֿיל מִיט: הָין ומפרנס.

אֳלֶע .צד׳ וֶעטֶען שְלָסכֶם, נָאר ירִיק דִיך צַד׳ אִיז נֶט.
ה. ה. יָיטן פָּון וָאנֶם צדִי־א נָקֶה, דִי זָאל דִיך צודֶיקֶען.

57

6. EAT AND BE WELL

Er est vi a ferd un kakt vi a foygl.

He eats like a horse and craps like a bird.

Fun shmole lokshn bekumt men nit kayn breytn tokhes.

You don't get a broad behind from thin noodles.

Az di kishke iz zat, freyt zikh der tokhes.

When your stomach is satisfied, your behind is overjoyed.

Der sod fun der mikve iz groys! — men geyt arayn un men pisht zikh oys, men kumt aroys, un men zogt nit oys.

The secret of the bathhouse is this: You go in, take a piss, come out feeling well, and don't ever tell.

Ver es pisht azoy oft vi a hunt, der iz frish un gezunt.

Pee as often as a hound, and you'll be fresh and sound.

עֶר עֶסט װי אַ פֿעֶרד און בֶּאקט װי אַ פֿינֶעל.

פֿון שׂמֹאלֶע לֹאקֶשׁן בֶּעקֹימט מֶען ניט קֵיין בּרֵייטֶען תַּחַת.

אַז די קֹישׁקֶע איז װאַט, פֿרֵייט זיך דֶער תַּחַת.
קֹישׁקֶע = p. kiszka

דֶער סֹוד פֿון דֶער מִקְוָה איז גְרֹויס! – מֶען גֵעהט אַרֵיין און מֶען פֿישׁט זיך אֹויס, מֶען קֹומט אַרֹויס, און מֶען זֹאנְט ניט אֹויס.

װעֶר עֶם פֿישׁט אַזוֹי אָפֿט װי אַ הוּנְד, דֶער איז פֿרִישׁ און געזוּנְד.

59

Az men pisht zikh oys, vert likhtiker in di oygn.

When you take a good piss, everything looks brighter.

Az men pisht klor, kakt men on dem dokter.

When you piss clear, you can crap on the doctor.

> That is, when the urine is clear, that's a sign one is healthy and doesn't need to see a doctor. (i.b.)

Ale eyvorim viln pishn, ober nor dem kleynem shtelt men aroys.

All your organs want to piss, but you only stick out the little one.

A pish on a forts iz vi a regn on a duner (oder:. . .vi a khasene on klezmer).

A piss without a fart is like rain without thunder (or:. . .like a wedding without a band).

An eygener forts shtinkt nit azoy vi a fremder.

Your own farts don't stink like someone else's.

Az men ken nit kakn, iz a forts aleyn oykh gut.

If you can't crap, a fart alone is also good.

אַז מען פֿישׁט זיך אויס, װערט ליכֿטיגער אין די אויגן.

אַז מען פֿישׁט קלאָר, קאַקט מען אָן דעם דאָקטאָר.

ר. ה. װען די השׁתָּנָה איז ריין, איז אַ סימָן, אַז מען איז געזונד און מען באַדאַרף ניט אַנצוקומען צו קיין דאָקטאָר.

אַלע אבֿרים װילען פֿישׁען, אָבער נאָר דעם קליינעם שׁטעלט מען אַרויס.

אַ פֿישׁ אָהן אַ פֿאָרץ איז װי װי אַ רעגען אָהן אַ דונער, (אָדער:... װי אַ חתונה אָהן כּלי־זמר.)

אַן אייגענער פֿאָרץ שׁטינקט ניט אַזוי, װי אַ פֿרעמדער.

אַז מען קען ניט קאַקען, איז אַ פֿאָרץ אַליין אויך גוט.

A yid kakt shabes mit blay.

A Jew craps lead on Saturday.

> Because the Sabbath meals lie heavy in the stomach. (i.b.)

Az men kakt zikh oys, vert gringer oyf dem hartsn.

A good crap makes your heart feel lighter.

Halt unter mit di hent di bakn, vest du gringer (laykhter) kakn.

Hold one hand under each cheek, take a crap without a squeak.

Leyg arayn in tokhes dem finger, vet dem kop vern gringer.

Stick your finger up your ass, make your head feel better fast.

Kakn, iz (baym khazn) nokh far dem davenen.

Crapping, for the Cantor, comes even before praying.

> A pious Jew, especially a cantor, sees to it that he purges himself before praying. (i.b.)

א יוד באַקט שׁבת מיט כְּלַי.

ווייל די שבּתדיגע באַאַבּלים ליגען זעהר שׁווער אין מאַנען.

אז מען באַקט זיך אוים, ווערט גרינגער אויף דעם האַרצען.

האַלט אונטער מיט די הענד די באַקען, וועסט דו גרינגער (לייכטער) באַקען.

לעג אַריין אין תָּחָת דעם פינגער, וועט דעם קאפ זאַט ווערען גרינגער.

באַקען איז (בּיים חַן) נאך פּאַר דעם דאַוונען.
א פרימעריה, בְּרָבּ א חַן, זעהט צו האָבּען נְקִיות זאַריך דאַוונען.

63

A knip in tokhes zol men zikh gebn un royt in ponem zol men zayn.

Give yourself a pinch on the behind and keep your cheeks rosy.

> That is, one should make every effort not to let the world see one's troubles. (i.b.)

Vos ker zikh on kadokhes mit'n tokhes?

What has a fever got to do with my behind?

> That's what a wife once asked her husband when she got angry at him because he swore at her — saying that she should come down with the ague. A patient is also supposed to have asked his doctor the same question when he prescribed an enema for his high fever. (i.b.)

A kane iz a gesheft vu men leygt tomid mer arayn vi men nemt aroys.

An enema is a business you put more into than you ever get out.

A kane shat oykh nit.

An enema can't hurt anything either.

> That's how you answer a person who is always asking: "What harm can that do?" (i.b.)

א קְנִיפּ אִין תָּחַת זָאל מֶען זִיךְ נֶעבֶּען אוּן רוּט אִין פָּנִים זָאל מֶען זַיִן.

ד. ה. מֶען זָאל זִיךְ מִיה נֶעבֶּען, זַיְנֶע צָרוֹת פַאר דֶער וֶועלְט וֶועלְט נִיט אַרוֹיסְצוּווַיַיזֶען.

וָואס קֶעהְר זִיךְ אָן בַּדִּחַת מִיטְן תָּחָת ?

אַזוֹי הָאט אַמָאל גֶעעְנטְפֶערְט אַ מַאן בַּיִין וַויַיבּ, וָואס דִי אִיז אוֹיף אִיהְם בְּרוֹגֶז גֶעווֶעזֶען, וַויַיל עֶר הָאט זִי גֶעשָׁאלְטֶען, זִי זָאל בֶּעקוּמֶען דָאס קַדַּחַת. — דָאם זָאל אוֹיךְ הָאבֶּען גֶעעְנטְפֶערְט אַ קְרַאנְקֶער דֶעם דָאקְטָאר, וָואס עֶר הָאט אִיהְם גֶעלָאזְט מאכֶען אַ קַאנֶע, וַויַיל עֶר הָאט גֶעהַאט שְׁטַאְרְקֶע הִיץ.

א קַאנֶע אִיז אַ גֶעשֶׁעפֶט. וואוּ מֶען לֶעגְט תָּמִיד מֶעהְר אַרַיִין, וַוי מֶען נֶעמְט אַרוֹים.

קַאנֶע = p. kanka

א קַאנֶע שַׁאדְט אוֹיךְ נִיט.

דָאס עֶנטְפֶערְט מֶען אַ מֶענשֶׁען, וָואס עֶר פְרֶעגְט תָּמִיד : וָואס קֶען דָאס שַׁאדֶען ?

65

Der zindiker mentsh, er muz esn un trinken, kakn (huren)
un shtinken.

Sinful man, he must eat and drink, crap (whore) and stink.

דֶער וִינְדִינֶער מֶענְשׁ, עֶר מוּז עֶסֶן אוּן טְרִינְקֶען, בַּאקֶען (הוּרֶען) אוּן שׁטִינְקֶען.

7. GETTING OLD

An alter man hot afile lib veykh fleysh, nor eyn shtikl vil er hobn hart, ken er es nit oysfirn.

An old man gets along fine on soft meat, but when he wants one piece hard — he can't manage it.

Oyf der elter vert klener dos taytl, un greser der baytl.

When you're old you get a smaller cock and need a larger jock.

Oyf der elter her oyf tsu zayn a khamur-eyzl, un nem dikh liber tsum gleyzl.

In your old age stop being an ass and learn to love the glass.

Zey hobn beyde in eyn gribl gepisht.

They both peed in the same little hole.

> Said of two bad boys who knew each other from **kheyder** and were lewd already then.

אין אַלטער מאַן האָט אַפֿילו ליב װײך פֿלײש, נאָר אײן שטיקעל װיל
ער האָבן האַרט, קען ער עס ניט אױספֿידהרֿען.

אױף דָער עלטער װערט קלײנער דאָס מײטעל, און גרעסער דער בײטעל.

אױף דָער עלטער הער אױף צו זײן אַ חמור־עזעל, און נעם דיך ליבֿער
צום גלעזעל.

זײ האָבן בײדע אין אײן גריבעל נעפישט.
זאָנט מען פֿון צװײ שלעכטע חבֿרים, װאָס זײ זענען שױן אין חדר בּעקאַנט און
אױסגעלאָסֿע: נעװעזען.

Ikh zol gevezn vartn, volt ikh nokh a moyd gevezn.

If I had gone and waited, I'd still be a virgin.

> This was said by an old, over-the-hill spinster who wasn't able to wait for a fully sanctified wedding, but took matters into her own hands. (i.b.)

Nit do di koykhes, vos moyd-vayz tsum kinder hobn!

I don't have the same strength to have kids that I had as a virgin.

> So complained a wife who had a child every year. (i.b.)

An alte moyd darf nit hobn nit kayn shtar un nit kayn keysef, nor dos drite.

An old maid doesn't need a deed and doesn't need silver, just the third thing.

> The third thing is understood here to be **biyo,** meaning sexual relations. (i.b.)

A yidene tut oyf eyn mol fir (oder finf) melokhes: zi kakt un pisht, arbet a zok, (kloybt shpeyner), un zogt brokhes.

An old biddy does four (or five) things at once: she craps and pisses, darns a sock, (picks splinters), and says her blessings.

אִיךְ זָאל גֶעװִינֶען װַארְטֶען, װָאלְט אִיךְ נָאךְ אַ מוֹיר נָעװִינֶען.

דָאס הָאט גֶעזָאנְט אַן אַלְטֶע אִיבֶּערְנֶעװַאקְסֶענֶע מוֹיד. װָאס זִי הָאט זִיךְ נִיט גֶעקֶענְט דֶערְװַארְטָען אוֹיף דֶער חוּפָּה כְּבַת מֹשֶׁה וְיִשְׂרָאֵל, אוּן הָאט זִיךְ פְרִיהֶער אָנ_עצֶה גֶעגֶעבֶּען.

נִיט דָא דִי כֹּחוֹת, װָאס מוֹיד־צַוַיין – צוּם קִינְדֶער הָאבֶּן!

אַזוֹי הָאט זִיךְ נֶעקְלָאגְט אַ װַײבֶּעל, װָאס זִי הָאט אַלֶע יָאהְר בֶּעקוּמֶען אַ קִינְד.

אַן אַלְטֶע מוֹיד דַארְף נִיט הָאבֶּען נִיט קַיין שְׁטַר אוּן נִיט קַיין כָּסֶף, נָאר דָאס דְרִיטֶע.

דָאס „דְרִיטֶע" פֶֿערְשְׁטֵעהְט מֶען דָא: בִּיאָה.

אַ יִדְעֶנֶע טְהוּט אוֹיף אַיין מָאל פִֿיעֶר (אֲחֵר: פִֿוּנְף) מְלָאכוֹת: זִי קָאקְט אוּן פִֿישְׁט אַרְבֵּיט אַ זַאק (קְלוֹיבְּט שְׁפֶּענֶער) אוּן זַאנְט בְּרָכוֹת.

An almone (oder: a yisoyme) iz a mitsve tsu kitslen, fun forn oder fun hintn.

It's a good deed to tickle a widow (or: an orphan girl) on her front or backside.

In der yugnt a hur, vert ofy der elter a gabitse.

A whore when young, pious in her old age.

A hur vert oyf der elter a tsitsis-shpinerin.

In her old age, a whore devotes herself to holy tassles.

A toyter ken nit fortsn (ober shtinken).

A dead man can't fart, only stink.

A mes iz poter fun piryo v'rivyo.

A corpse is all through with "be fruitful and multiply."

אַן אַלְמָנָה (אָדער: אַ יְתוֹמָה) איז אַ מִצְוָה צו קוצלען, פֿון פֿאָרן אָדער
פֿון הינטען.

װײַל עס איז אַ מִצְוָה זײ מְשַׂמֵּחַ צו זײַן, דָעריבָּער מָען מיט זײ קאטאָװעס טרײַבּען.

אין דָער יוגענד אַ הוּר, װערט אויף דָער עלטער אַ נבֿיאיסטע.

אַ הוּר װערט אויף דָער עלטער אַ ציצית־שפּינערין.

אַ טויטער קָען ניט פֿאָרצען (אָבער שטינקען.)

אַ מֵת איז פָטוּר פֿון פִּרְיָה וְרִבְיָה.

73

8. TALMUDIC TAKEOFFS

Piryo v'rivyo iz di beste mitsve (nor fil koyakh muz men tsun ir hobn).

"Be fruitful and multiply" is the best commandment, but you need the strength to live up to it.

Vu odem—horoshon hot nit gepisht, dort ken kayn groyse shtot nit zayn.

Where Adam didn't pee, no great city can ever be.

> What is meant is that a spot that does not lie next to some great waterway cannot develop into a great city. The folk say the following: that the great lakes, oceans, and rivers were created from water which Adam made. (i.b.)

Far vos hot odem un khave tsugedekt di mayse mit a blat, ven keyner hot zey nit gezen?

Why did Adam and Eve cover their business with leaf, if there was nobody to see them?

פְּרִיָה וְרִבְיָה אִיז דִי בֶּעסטע מִצְוָה (נָאר פִיל כֹּחַ מוז מֶען צוּרִינְ־אַיהְר הָאבֶּען).

וואוּ אָדָם־הָרִאשׁוֹן הָאט נִיט גֶעפִישׁט, דָארְט קֶען קֵיין נְרוֹיסֶע שְׁטָאדְט נִיט זַיין.

קֶען מֵיינְט אַן אָרְט, וָואס עֶס לִיגְט נִיט בַּיי קֵיין נְרוֹיס וַואסֶער, קֶען קֵיין נְרוֹיסֶע שְׁטָאדְט נִיט וֶוערְען. דָאס פָאלְק זָאגְט נֶעמְלִיךְ, אַז דִי נְרוֹיסֶע טַייכֶען נֶעמֶען נֶעזָאיצֶען פוּן דֶעם וַואסֶער, וָואס אָדָם־הָרִאשׁוֹן הָאט נֶעלָאזְט.

פָאר וָואס הָאט אָדָם אוּן חַוָה צִיגֶעֶרְעקְט דִי מַעֲשֶׂה מִיט אַ בְּלָאט, וֶוען קֵיינֶער הָאט זֵיי נִיט נֶעזֶעהֶען?

75

Zi hot gute moyshe v'aharondlekh.

She's got good Moses and Aaronses.

> Said of a woman with full breasts. In the Song of Songs there occurs the phrase "shney shodayikh" — two breasts. The writer in the Midrash (commentary) is ashamed to give the true translation of these two words, so he says all that is meant by "shney shodayyikh" is Moses and Aaron. (i.b.)

Der grester khesorn bay a meydl iz der ku-seykhl (oder: der seykhl fun a bas koyen).

The greatest fault a girl can have is to have "cow-sense" (or: the sense of a Cohan's daughter).

> That is, when she misbehaves. "Cow-sense" (kuseykhl) is a pun on the Biblical verse: ". . .ki seykhl liznoys (because she began to prostitute herself)." (i.b.)

"Labris habeyt" — tsum bris a bet — "v'al teyfen l'yeytser" — un drey dikh nit far dem yeytser.

Get a bed for the bris — and don't resist the urge.

> This is how an uncouth young man once translated this Biblical verse: "Follow the covenant, and do not let temptation move you." (i.b.)

76

ווי האָט נוטע משֶׁה וְאַהֲרֹן/דְלֶעך.

פֿון אַ נְקֵבָה מיט פֿילע פּײנטען. — אין שיר־הַשִׁירים (ז. ה.) קומט פֿיר דער פָּסוק
„…שְׁנֵי שָׁדַיִך. דער מדרש שעטט זיך אַרויסצוזאָגען דעם אֶמֶתן מײטש פֿון די צְוויי
ווערטער זאָגט ער, אַז מען מיינט נאָר מיט „שְׁנֵי שָׁדַיִך‎" משֶׁה און אַהֲרן.

דער גרעסטער חִסָרוֹן בּײ אַ מיידעל איז דער קוה־שֵׂכֶל (אָדער:… דער
שֵׂכֶל פֿון אַ בַת־כֹּהֵן.)

ה. ה. ווען זי פֿירהט זיך שְׁלֶעכט אױף. — „קוה־עֵגֶל‎" איז אַ װאָרטשפּיל מיט דעם
פָּסוק „…כִּי תָּחֵל לִזְנוֹת.‎"

„לִכְרִית הַבֵּט‎" — צום בְּרִית אַ בֶּעטעט. „וְאַל תִּפֶּן לְיֵצֶר‎, און דְרָעה דיך
ניט פֿאַר דעם יֵצֶר.
אַזױ האָט אַמאָל אַ נְזאָפֿער־יונג נֶעטײַטשט דעם פָּסוק.

"Mi yidme lokh, mi yishve lokh, v'mi ya'arokh lokh" – *A lokh iz a lokh.*

A hole is a hole.

> Parody of the Biblical verse: "Who has thy countenance, who is thy equal, and who has thy value". (eds.)

"M'mikhnosayim yotso sod," vozhe makhst du fun a forts aza groys vezn?

"The pants gave out a little secret"; why such a big fuss over a fart?

> A travesty of the proverb: "Nikhnas yayin, yotso sod (wine goes in, the secret comes out)." (i.b.)

"Al khet shekhotonu l'fonekho bividas z'nis" – *Es iz ober fort zeyer zis!*

"For a sin that I sinned before you with prostitutes" – But it's still very sweet!

> So a man once beat his breast in repentance during Kol Nidre. (i.b.)

"Osur-khazir" iz kayn shvue; "kush in tokhes" iz kayn klole.

"God forbid" doesn't make a pledge; "Kiss my ass" is no real curse.

„מִי יִדְמֶה לָּךְ, מִי יִשְׁוֶה לָּךְ וּמִי יַעֲרָךְ לָּךְ" – אַ לָאךְ אִיז אַ לָאךְ.

„מִמַּכְנְסַיִם יָצָא סוֹד" ווָאס־זְשֶׁע מַאכְסְט דּוּ פֿוּן אַ פֿאַרְץ אַזַא נְרוֹיס ווֶיעֶן?
טְרַאכְטֶעטֶע אוֹיף דֶעם שְׁפָּרְיקוֹנַארְט ,,נִכְנַס יַיִן, יָצָא סוֹד".

„עַל חֵטְא שֶׁחָטָאנוּ לְפָנֶיךָ בְּוֶעֲדַת זְנוּת' – ,,עֶס אִיז אָבֶּער פֿאַרְט זֶעהֶר זִים!
אַזוֹי הָאט זִיךְ אַקָאל אַ יִּד נֶעשְׁלָאגֶען אִין הַאַרְץ אַרַיין בַּיים ,,עַל־חֵטְא צוּ פֿאַל־נִדְרֵי.

,,אֶסִיר־חֲזִיר' אִיז קֵיין שְׁבוּעָה, ,,קוּשׁ אִין תָּחַת' אִיז קֵיין קְלָלָה.

"Lag b'omer" – lig bay mir.

"Lag B'omer" – lie with me.

> So the young men tease the girls – because at Lag
> B'omer there are many weddings. (i.b.)

Vi der purim, azoy iz di leyl-shmurim.

As at Purim, so on the first night of Passover.

> That's how the women figure out if they'll be
> menstruating on the first night of Passover, and
> whether or not they will be able to be at their
> husbands' side. Between Purim and Passover is exactly
> four weeks. (i.b.)

Kush mikh, vu di yidn hobn geruht!

Kiss me where the Jewish people once rested.

> That is, on the behind. One of the rest stations of the
> Jews in the wilderness was called Tokhes. (i.b.)

*"Loy seyvoyshi v'loy sikolmi" – Kvetsh dikh nit un
kak nit.*

Don't creak and don't crap.

> A coarse rendition of the verse "Be not fearful nor
> ashamed", in "Come Beloved", a hymn sung to
> greet the Sabbath. (i.b.)

„ל"ג בְּעוֹמֶר׳ – לִין בַּי מִיר!

אַזוי פֶּאַרשֶעפֶּען די יוּנְגֶע לַײט די מֵײדֶעלֶעך, וַוייל אים ל"ג בְּעוֹמֶר שְׁפֶּעלֶט מָען אַ סַך חוּפּֿוֹת.

וְוִי דֶער פּוּרים, אַזוי אִיז די לֵיל־שִׁמּוּרים.

די וַוייבֶּער פֶּאַרעקֶענֶען אַזוי, צִי זַיי וֶועלֶען נִיט בֶּעקוּמֶען די וָוֶוסְט צוּ דֶער „עַרְשְׁטֶער סֵדֶר־נאַכְט אוּן צִי זַיי וֶועלֶען קֶענֶען זַיין אַ מַלְכָּה, וַוייל צְווֹישֶׁען פּוּרים אוּן פֶּסַח זֶענֶען פּוּנְקְט פֶֿער וָואכֶען.

קוּש מִיך, וָואִי די יוּדֶען הָאבֶּען גֶערוִיהְט!

ה. ה. אִין אָהֹר אַיַין, מֶען בֶּעוִיזְט זִיך נֶעמְלִיך אוֹיסְן פֶּסוּק: וַיִּחַט כְּתָחַת.

„לֹא תֵבוֹשִׁי וְלֹא תִכָּלְמִי׳ – קְנֶעטְשׁ דִיך נִיט אוּן קַאק נִיט.

שֶׁעֶרְצְהַאפֶּטֶע אִיבֶּערזֶעצוּנְג פֿוּן דֶעם פָּסוּק אִין לְכָה־דוֹדִי.

Far tashmish shteyt er, nokh tashmish ligt er.

Before doing it, he stands; after doing it he rests.

> Tashmish is a ritual prayer. (eds.)

Dots der soykher, puts der mekler.

Dick the merchant, Prick the broker.

> Said when two fools want to carry out a business deal. Based on a verse in a song sung to accompany the ending of the Sabbath: "Dots ha'soykher bir'-oysoy. . ." (i.b.)

Rik zikh, vu halt ikh do?

Slide over; now, where was I?

> A travesty of the Biblical verse: "Rigzu v'al tekhta'u (be angry but do not sin)". The man asks his wife this when they lie in bed in the dark. (i.b.)

A poroykhes on gleklekh un m'shoyr'rim on shmeklekh iz kayn yidishe shul nit.

A Torah curtain without little gongs, and a choir without little dongs, is no Jewish synagogue.

> This is how the Orthodox Jews deride the reform synagogues for having instituted organs and womens' choirs. (i.b.)

פֿאַר תַּשְׁמִישׁ שְׁטֶעהְט עֶר, נאָךְ תַּשְׁמִישׁ לִיגְט עֶר.

דָן דָער סוֹחֵר, פֿאַן דָער מֶעקְלֶער.

זאַן צְוַויי שְׁלִים-מַזַלְנִיקֶעס וִוילֶען אוֹיסְפֿיהְרֶען אַ נֶעשֶׂעפֿט. — בֶּעצִיהְט זִיךְ אוֹיךְ אַ פֿסוּק
אִין דִי זְכִירוֹת לְמוֹצָאֵי שַׁבָּת: דָן הַסוֹחֵר בְּיָאוֹתוֹ...

ריק זִיךְ, וואוּ האַלְט אִיךְ דָא?

טְראַנְסְפֿעֶנֶע פֿון דֶעם פֿסוּק: „רְנָנוּ וְאַל תַּחֲטָאוּ." דאָס פֿרֶעגְט דָער מאַן דאָס וַוייב, זַיי
זַיי לִיגֶען אִין בֶּעטְט אִין דֶער פֿינְסְטֶער.

אַ פֿרוּכְת אָהְן גְלֶעקְלֶעךְ, אוּן מְשׁוֹרְרִים אָהְן שְׁמֶעקְלֶעךְ אִיז קַיין יוּדִישֶׁע
שׁוּהְל נִיט.
אַזוֹי שֶׁפֶּעטֶען דִי פֿרוּמֶע יוּדֶען פֿון דִי רֶעפֿאָרְמִירְטֶע סִינאַגאָגֶען, וֶועלְכֶע האָבֶּען בַּיי זִיךְ
אַיינְגֶעפֿיהְרְט אָרְגֶעל אוּן פֿרוֹיֶוענְקאָר.

9. WIT AND WISDOM

Mit eyn tokhes ken men nit tantsn oyf tsvey khasenes.

With one behind you can't dance at two weddings.

Az men hot nor in zin bromfn un kurves, geyt men tsum sof naket un borves.

If all that you're after is loose women and booze, you wind up in the end without clothing or shoes.

Vintshn un kakn iz alts eyns.

Wishing and crapping are just the same.

> That is, both are of the same value. About this, however, folks remark that the saying is not true, because if you wish into one hand and crap into the other, the latter always stays full. (i.b.)

Tsum vinshn un tsum fartsn bedarf men nit fun'm bet oyftsushteyn.

For wishes and farts, you don't have to get out of bed.

מיט אײן תָּחַת קֶען מֶען ניט טַאנצֶען אוֹיף צְװײ חֲתֻנוֹת.

אַז מֶען האָט נאָר אין זין בְּרָאנְפֶן אוּן קוּרְוֶעם, גֶעהְט מֶען צוּם־סוֹף
נאַקֶט אוּן בָּארְוֶועם.
קוּרְוֶע = p. kurwa

װינְשֶׁען אוּן קאַקֶען איז אַלֶץ אײנְם.
ד. ה. בײדֶע האָבֶּען אײן װעָרְמֶה. דאַרוֹיף בֶּעמֶערְקְט דאָס פאָלְק אַז דאָס שְׁפְּרִיכְװאָרְט
איז גִים אֱמֶת, װָארוּם װֶען מֶען װינְשְׁט אין אײן האַנְד אוּן מֶען קאַקְט אין דֶער אַנְדֶערֶער
האַנְד, בְּלײבְּט די לֶעצְטֶע תָּמִיד פֿוּל.

צוּם װינְשֶׁען אוּן צוּם פאַרְצֶען בֶּעדאַרְף מֶען ניט פֿוּנֶם בֶּעטְ
אוֹיפְצוּשְׁטֶעהֶען.

85

Vilst fleysh? — Khap dikh on baym tokhes!

You want meat? — Grab your behind.

> In this way a mother yells at a child who wants another
> piece of meat. (i.b.)

Vos iz di maynse? — Di maynse iz bavaksn.

What's up? — What's up is hairy.

> That's how you answer someone who is always asking:
> "What's up?" (i.b.)

A shadkh'n iz a kurve-mekler.

A matchmaker is a pimp.

A kort iz vi a hur.

A card is like a whore.

> That is: False and untrue. (i.b.)

A ganef iz kayn bruder, a kurve iz kayn shvester.

A thief is no brother, a whore is no sister.

A vort un a forts ken men nit tsuriknemen.

Words and farts can't be taken back.

וִילְסְט פְּלֵייש? – חַאפּ דִיךְ אָן בַּיים תָּחַת!

אַזוֹי שְׁרַייט אַ בֵּייזֶע מוּטֶער אוֹיף דָעם קִינְד, וָואס עֶס פָּערלַאנְגְט נָאךְ אַ שְׁטִיקֶעל פְּלֵייש.

וָואס אִיז דִי מַעֲשֶׂה? – דִי מַעֲשֶׂה אִיז בֶּעווָאקְסֶען.

דָאס עֶנְטְפֶערְט מֶען אַ מֶענְשֶׁען, וָואס פְרֶעגְט תָּמִיד: "וָואס אִיז דִי מַעֲשֶׂה?"

אַ שַׁדְכָן אִיז אַ קוּרְוֶוע-מָעקְלֶער.

אַ קָארְט אִיז ווִי אַ הוּר.

ד. ה. פַאלְש אוּן אוּמְגֶעטְרַיי.

אַ גַּנָב אִיז קֵיין בְּרוּדֶער, אַ קוּרְוֶוע אִיז קֵיין שְׁוֶועסְטֶער.

קוּרְוֶוע = p. kurwa

אַ וָוארְט אוּן אַ פָארְץ קֶען מֶען נִיט צוּרִיקְנֶעמֶען.

87

A klole on beyner? − Ot, kush mikh in tokhes arayn!

A tender curse? − Here, kiss my ass!

A puts shteyt, ober di tsayt sheyt nit!

A prick stands, but time doesn't.

> In this way, for example, one scolds a slowpoke servant who stands in one place and won't move. (i.b.)

Red mit a shvants khokhmes!

Try to talk sense to a prick!

> When you ask someone why he has so many children, he answers that you can't reason with the evil urge, because: "Lasciviousness has no master." (i.b.)

A goyish petsl iz vi a shpitsik mitsl, a yidish petsl iz vi a kapelush.

A Gentile rod is like a dunce cap, a Jewish rod is like a derby.

A mitsve, vi a shiker'n goy pishn tsu firn.

Some good deed, − like finding a drunk Gentile a place to piss.

> That is, it's no big thing. (i.b.)

אַ קללה אָהן בײַנער – אָט, קוש מיך אין תּחת אַרײַן!

אָט = p. ot

אַ פּאָן שטעהט, אָבער די צײַט שטעהט ניט!

אַזוי בײַנעמט מען זיך למשל אויף אַ סעודה אַ קריבער, װאָס ער שטעהט אין רידרט זיך ניט פֿונים אָרט.

רעד מיט אַ שװאַנץ חכמות!

אַז מען פֿרעגט אײנעם, פֿאַר־װאָס ער האָט אַזוי פֿיל קינדער, ענטפֿערט ער, אַז מיט יצר־הרע קען מען קיין חכמות ניט רעדן, װאָרום: "אין אַפּיטרופּוס לעריות."

אַ גוי'ש פֿעצעל איז װי אַ שפּיצינ'ס מיצעל, אַ ייִדיש פֿעצעל איז װי אַ קאַפּעלוש.

קאַפּעלוש = p. kapelusz

אַ מצוה, װי אַ שכּורן ניט פּישען צו פֿאַרהדרען.

ד. ה. עס איז ניט קיין זעהר גרויסע מצוה.

Az men shpilt zikh bay nakht mit fayer, bapisht men zikh in bet.

Play with fire at night, and you're sure to wet your bed.

> This is what one tells children to keep them from playing with fire. (i.b.)

Az men pisht a tseylem, peygert a galekh.

If you piss on a cross, a priest dies.

> That's what schoolboys say in Russia. (i.b.)

A yid iz vi a vants: tshepet men im, bayst er; tsekvetsht men im, shtinkt er.

A man is like a bedbug; mess with him, he bites; squash him, he stinks.

Az eyn yid shtelt zikh pishn, shteln zikh di ibrige oykh.

When one Jew stands to piss, the rest stand with him.

> What is meant is the solidarity of the Jews: that is, "one responsible for the other." In addition, they say as a joke that, therefore, the Jews dare not go to war, because they will all get up to go at the same time, and meanwhile the enemy will capture the town. (i.b.)

Az a yidish vaybl shloft mit a goy, kumt aroys a fertiger m'shumed.

If a Jewish woman sleeps with a Gentile, out comes a ready-made convert.

אַז מֶען שְׁפִּילְט זִיךְ בַּיי נַאכְט מִיט מִיט פַיֶער, בֶּעפִּישְׁט מֶען זִיךְ אִין בֶּעטְט.

אַזוֹי זָאגְט מֶען פִֿיר דִי קִינְדֶער, כְּדֵי זֵיי זָאלֶען זִיךְ נִיט שְׁפִּילֶען מִיט פַיֶער.

אַז מֶען פִֿישְׁט אַ צֶלֶם, פֶּגֶר'ט אַ גַלָח.

אַזוֹי זָאגֶען דִי חֶדֶר-יוּנְגְלֶעךְ אִין רוּסְלַאנְד.

אַ יוּד אִיז וְוִי אַ וַואנְץ: טְשֶׁעפֶּעט מֶען אִיהְם, בַּייסְט עֶר, צֶעקְוְועטְשְׁט
מֶען אִיהְם, שְׁטִינְקְט עֶר.
טְשֶׁעפֶּען = p. zaczepić

אַז אֵיין יוּד שְׁטֶעלְט זִיךְ פִֿישֶׁען, שְׁטֶעלֶען זִיךְ דִי אִיבְּרִיגֶע אוֹיךְ.
סָאן וְוִיל דֶערְמִיט זָאגֶען, אַז אַלֶע יוּדֶען זֶענֶען סָאלִידַארִישׁ ד. ה. עֲרֵבִים זָה בָּזֶה.
אוֹיסֶערְדֶעם זָאגְט מֶען דָאס אוֹיף קַאטָאוֶועס, אַז דֶערִיבֶּער סָאלֶען דִי יוּדֶען נִיט אִין דֶער
סְלָחָה אַרֵיין גֵעהֶען, וָזאַרוּם אַלֶע וְואלְטֶען זִיךְ אוֹיף אֵיין סָאל נֶעטְצֶעלְט מַשְׁטֵין זַיין,
אוּן דֶערְוֵוייל וָואלְט דֶער שׂוֹנֵא דִי שְׁטַאדְט אֵיינְגֶענֶעמֶען.

אַז אַ (יוּדִישׁ) וַויייבֶּעל שְׁלָאפְֿט מִיט אַ גּוֹי, קוּמְט אַרוֹיס אַ פֶֿערְטִינֶער
מַמְזֶר.

Ven a royter sholft mit a shvartser, kumen aroys shpakovate kinder.

When redhair sleeps with blackhair, the children come out dappled.

Kak, az der tokhes is tsu!

Go shit, when your ass is shut!

> That is, how is one to finish something without the wherewithal? (i.b.)

Kaker, makh dir harts!

Shitter, take heart!

> One says this to somebody who is afraid of every little thing. (i.b.)

Gey vayter kakn!

Go on with your crap!

> That's what you say to someone who has become lewd. (i.b.)

Az men hot nit vos zu tun, iz kakn oykh an arbet.

If you've got nothing to do, crapping is also work.

װען אַ רױטער שלאָפֿט מיט אַ שװאַרצער קומען אַרױס שפּאַקאַװאַטע קינדער.

שׁפּאַקאַװאַטע == p. szpakowaty

קאַק, אַו דער תָּהַת איז צו!

ה. ה. װי זאָל מען אַ זאַך אױסצִיהֶען, װען די מִיטֶעל פֿעהלֶען﬩

קאַקער, מאַך דיר האַרץ!

זאָגט מען צוּ־נ־אײנעם, װאָס ער האָט מורא פֿאַר דער סינדסטער זאַך.

נעה װײטער קאַקן!

זאָגט מען צוּ־נ־אײנעם, װאָס ער איז לעסטיג נעטאָרען.

אַו מען האָט ניט װאָס צו טהון, איז קאַקען אױ׳ך אַן אַרבײם.

93

Az got vet mikh derfreyen, vel ikh oykh mit'n tokhes dreyen.

If God gave me a little luck, I'd also shake my butt.

> So says a poor girl who still hopes to make a rich match. (i.b.)

Oyf a fremdn tokhes iz gut tsu patshn.

It's better to spank someone else's behind.

Az men shmayst in tokhes, geyt es in kop arayn.

Beat the behind and it goes right to the head.

> That is: You long remember the offense for which you were whipped. (i.b.)

Az men shmayst in tokhes, veynen di oygn.

Spank the behind and the eyes cry.

Oyf a greytn tokhes iz gut a kane tsu makhn.

When the behind is ready, that's the time to give an enema.

Beser fun der ergster ganz der tokhes, eyder fun'm bestn khazn der haldz.

Better the behind of the worst goose, than the neck of the best cantor.

אַז נאָט וועט מיך דערפֿרײַען, וועל איך אויך מיטן תָּחַת דרעהען.

זאָנט אָן אָרֶעם מײדֶעל, וואָס די האָסט נאָך אַ_רײַנען שׁידוך צו טאָן.

אויף אַ פֿרעמדֶען תָּחַת איז נוט צו פּאטשֶען.

אַז מֶען שׁמײַסט אין תָּחַת, נֶעהט עס אין קאָפּ אַרײַן.

ה. ה. מֶען נֶעדֶענקט לאַנג די באַטָאים, פֿאַר וועלכֶע מֶען האָט אָפּגֶעשׁטיסֶען.

אַו מֶען שׁמײַסט אין תָּחַת, ווײַנֶען די אויגֶען.

אויף אַ גרײַטֶען תָּחַת איז נוט אַ קאַנֶע צו מאַכֶען.

קאַנֶע ‎= p. kanka

בֶעסֶער פֿון דֶער ערנסטֶער נאַנו דֶער תָּחַת, אײדֶער פֿונ'ם בֶעסטֶען חָן דֶער האָלו.

95

Er lernt an altn tatn kinder makhn!

He's trying to teach an old dad how to make babies.

> So an elder answers when a young whipper-snapper wants to instruct him. (i.b.)

Az men shtekt arayn in alemen di noz, shmekt men tinef.

Poke your nose into everyone's business, you'll find it stinks.

Fun drek ken men kayn koyletsh mit flekhten.

You can't roll strudel out of shit.

Geforn, geforn, a tokhes gekumen!

Rode and rode, and came back an ass!

> When someone comes back from a trip and has not successfully accomplished his business. (i.b.)

Vil er, vil zi nit, vil zi, vil er nit, viln beyde, falt arop der firhang.

He wants, she doesn't; she wants, he doesn't; they both want, down comes the curtain.

> In this way a Jew once described his first time at the theater. (i.b.)

עֶר קֶערְט אָן אַלְטֶן טאטֶן קוֹנְדֶער מאבָּען!

דאָס עַנְטְפֶּעֶרְט אַ פֿאָטֶער, ווֶען אַ יוֹנְגֶער מאָנְטְשִיק ווִיל אִיהְם מַדְרִיךְ זַיין.

אַז מֶען שטֶעקְט אַרַיין אִין אַלֶעמֶען דִי נאָז, שמָעקְט מֶען מֶען סִינָת.

פֿון הֶרֶעק קֶען מֶען קֶיין קִילֶעטְש נִיט פֿלֶעכְטֶן.

קִילֶעטְש = ‏;p. kołacz

נֶעפֿאָהְרֶען, נֶעפֿאָהְרֶען, אַ תִּחָת נֶעקוּמֶען!

ווֶען אַיינֶער קוֹמְט צוּרִיק פֿוּנִים ווֶעג, אוּן האָט נִיט אוֹיסְנֶעפֿיהְרְט זַיין נֶעשֶׁעֿטֿ.

ווִיל עֶר, ווִיל זִי נִיט, ווִיל זִי, ווִיל עֶר נִיט, ווִילֶען בֵּיידֶע, פֿאַלְט אַרָאב דָער פֿיִרהאָנְג.

דאָס האָט אַמאָל דֶערְצֶעהְלְט אַ יוּד, ווֹאָס עֶר אִיז נֶעווֶעזֶען דאָס עֶרְשְׁטֶע מאָל אִין טֶעאַטֶער.

97

Di bobe zol hobn a shmekele, volt zi gevezn a zeydele.

If grandma had a wee dicky, she'd be a wee grandpa.

די באַבע זאָל האָבן אַ שמעקעלע, וואָלט זי געוועון אַ זיידעלע.

p. babka = בּאַבּע

4048858

Made in the USA
Lexington, KY
16 December 2009